STARTING
POINT

STARTING POINT

HOW TO CREATE WEALTH THAT LASTS

KEVIN L. MATTHEWS II

BuildingBread-Page Press

Dallas • New York • Tulsa

Starting Point
How to Create Wealth That Lasts

Copyright 2014 by Kevin L. Matthews II

ISBN: 978-0-692-23610-9

Cover design by Lauren McMillan

Typesetting by wordzworth.com

SPECIAL SALES

Books are available at a special discounts for bulk purchases for sales promotions or premiums. For more information write to BuildingBread-Page Press Books, *Kevin@BuildingBread.com*.

Paw-Paw this is for you.

Contents

Introduction

On April 28, 2011 around 8 p.m. in New York City, a man by the name of Cam Newton walked across the stage of Radio City Music Hall and became a multimillionaire. The news came as a shock to no one. It was not a matter of luck that he earned this type of wealth; it was the result of blood, sweat, and tears. In an instant, Cam went from college student to fame and fortune.

Meanwhile, Jeffery Jones watched the event while helping his wife grade papers at their home near Atlanta, Georgia. Jones, 57, is the owner of a mobile home park and loves to travel when his wife is not teaching, during the summer. In contrast, Cam was the 2011 Heisman Trophy winner and the number one pick in the 2011 NFL draft by the Carolina Panthers. In July, Cam signed his rookie contract, guaranteeing him $22 million. What do these men and their peers have in common?

Both are millionaires now but chances are, only one will remain wealthy in the future. There are more millionaire teachers in the U.S. than there are millionaire professional athletes. Dr. Thomas J. Stanley, author of *The Millionaire Mind* and *The Millionaire Next Door*, studied the affluent population of the U.S. in the 1990s. His research found that there were 3.5 million millionaire households and that about 95 percent of those homes had a net worth between $1 million and $10 million. What's more, *Sports Illustrated* estimated in April 2012 that 78 percent of NFL athletes would go bankrupt. It is obvious that the average millionaire is not an athlete, but what may not be as obvious is a clear picture of what wealth truly is and why so many people are left out.

The average millionaire is male, about 54 years old, married with three kids. The number one occupation for those million-aires' wives? Teacher. The "real" housewives of Atlanta have almost no "real" wealth. It's these exact misconceptions that weigh down our finances and affect us in ways we don't even realize. It's finally time to fix our finances, inside and out.

We are often told that education is important. Eat your vegetables, do your homework, go to college, and get a good job: that's pretty much the formula for the American dream, right? The first problem with this widely held axiom is that we rarely follow good advice. It is too boring, too simple, and it works too well for the majority of Americans to follow. We want instant gratification, flair, and huge results. Take the first statement: "Eat your veggies." At some point, our parents forced this on us. It is something we know we should do, and we know for a fact that it will help improve our lives. Yet, regardless of that simple, three-word command, the obesity rate has steadily climbed over the last few decades. Sure, if you want, you can blame it on McDonald's, Burger King, or whatever else may be calling your name late at night, but the bottom line is still the same: *you* choose to eat there and *you* choose to eat unhealthy options.

What's even worse is that, when we gain weight, we know exactly how to lose it: eat less, exercise more. Another simple, four-word phrase. But do we follow it? No. As a nation, we are too concerned about the fast and trendy way to lose weight. Six-pack abs in six days and countless crash diets might work for a little while but will have you back in the mirror bigger than you were when you began.

Financial problems are not always just financial: they're also mental and emotional. Just like our bad food habits, it is not always the food that's the issue; it's more of a deficiency in the department of self-control. On a large scale, our problems can be traced back to our education: we are taught how to count, multiply, add, subtract, and divide. When you get to college, especially in business courses, you're taught to do the same – but for someone else's money. Those courses are called accounting and finance.

At what point were you taught to manage your own money? At what point were you taught how to invest, save and retire properly? Chances are, you *weren't* taught in school. In 2010, USA Today reported that only 15 states offer a personal finance course, and only 13 of those states require it for high school graduation[1].

Clearly, it wasn't taught in school, but what about at home? In 2011, Capital One and ING Direct USA researched the spending habits and financial education of 12-17-year-olds. They found that only 17 percent claimed that they knew how to manage their money well and that only 31 percent of parents would consider themselves excellent financial role models.

Worst of all, more than half of all teens will learn about financial topics at home (52 percent). [2]So, you may learn about money at home – half of us do – but with only a handful of parents who consider themselves good teachers.

And here we are, a nation of short-term thinkers, too often with college degrees and major credit card debt – great jobs and big salaries, but even bigger spending habits. We're great

---

[1] Malcolm, H. (2012, April 24). Millennials struggle with financial literacy. *USATODAY.COM.*

[2] Teens & Plastic: A Quarter Of U.S. Teens Don't Know The Difference Between Debit And Credit. (2012, July 21).

customers and consumers, but we're terrible at conservation and preparation. By now, you know exactly how we got here, and it's my mission to show you exactly how to get out.

My goal for this book is to give you a clear and concrete plan for building wealth and an even clearer picture of what wealth really looks like. I know the cycle of the rat race, student loan debt, and poor financial decisions personally, and I know how much of a burden it can be every day. This book is for the college kid who is worried that what she is majoring in won't make enough money. This is for the newly married couple who wants more for their kids. It's for the six-figure executive who still can't seem to make enough money to cover the bills.

I am the founder and CEO of BuildingBread; my company helps individuals learn to manage their money and budget on their own. Essentially, my company helps fill in the knowledge gaps that parents and schools do not when it comes to finances. I've been fortunate enough to travel coast to coast, speaking with people in their homes, high schools and colleges, and the stories remain the same. I am also a seventh grade math teacher and a member of the 2012 Teach for America Corps. Each and every day, I see how the cycle of financial mishaps begin and manifest into what will become terrible financial habits.

Fortunately, I have the opportunity to intervene and stress the importance of budgeting through math, but I cannot help but cringe at the millions of other students in the country who do not have the resources nor role models to guide their steps.

I've found that many people are afraid of the topic of money. The most common reason is that it is too telling. Like a scale, there is no way to hide from the truth. No one wants to hear that their habits will create problems in their future, nor do they want to hear that their lavish lifestyle isn't that lavish (when they can barely cover the bills). The second fear about money conversations is that it's too complex. Stocks, bonds, dividends, derivatives, 401(k)s, tax law, and the like will kill any conversation among those who do not already have a working knowledge on the topic.

I want to address these two fears. My promise to you is that my message will be clear and concise. I will be fair and warn you, though: I may say some things that will shock you and wake you up. Deal with it. These statements have been made on purpose.

My goal is to break the habits and beliefs that are impeding your progress to financial independence. Sometimes, you have to throw a few punches if you plan to break things.

Lastly, this book will largely serve to create a new class of truly wealthy individuals. The words "truly wealthy" mean that you're not dependent upon your income or paycheck. True wealth doesn't reference how much you're bringing in, but how much you have left when all the bills have been paid off. True wealth doesn't die with you but is passed on from generation to generation.

As you read, I strongly urge you to highlight, underline, fold the pages, and scribble in the margins. Don't leave this book the way you found it.

Let's get to it!

—KM

CHAPTER ONE

Living the Financial Lie

It is rarely comforting to discover a lie, and it often seems that, the longer the lie evades the truth, the more shocking and dangerous the lie becomes. Webster's Dictionary defines, a lie as "something intended or serving to convey a false impression." Keep this definition in mind throughout this chapter.

Between 1999-2005, Lance Armstrong was a true American hero. Not only was he one of the greatest athletes in history, but he simultaneously became one of the best known cancer survivors in the process. Lance won a record seven Tour de France titles during his career. Three years prior to his historic title accomplishment, in October of 1996, he was diagnosed with testicular cancer that had spread to both his brain and lungs and was told that he would have to undergo chemotherapy. By February 1997, Lance was declared cancer-free, resumed his training, and made history.

But there is more to his story. In 2001, he announced his (first) retirement, but not without suspicion and doubt. Lance was facing investigation of doping during his cycling run. Pressure mounted, and the evidence continued to pile up. In

2012, he was stripped of his record seven titles. Lance has displayed a false impression. The professional cycling career of Lance Armstrong was a lie. When you wrap yourself up in a false lifestyle, take shortcuts, and ignore common sense, you will get caught sooner or later – in sports and in life, but especially with your money. Perhaps one of the worst feelings surrounding lies isn't being lied to, but actually buying into that lie at full price and embracing it as your reality.

In the summer of 2010, I slowly uncovered the reality of wealth and why it has evaded so many. That year, I had the opportunity to intern with one of the largest investment management firms in the country. Only a sophomore in college, I thought that this was my dream. Since I was a kid, I knew I wanted to be a businessman; crayon contracts and blueprints replaced my coloring books as I converted my Rose Art purple plastic briefcase into my portable office. Going to the Big Apple from Tulsa, OK, was the biggest thing for me. It was what I had been dreaming of my whole life. I was done with the part-time gas station job and the silver nametag that read "Kevin since 2007." It was finally my time to make it big.

I was placed in the asset allocation division. Having just finished my second year of college, I hadn't taken any courses in Economics yet, and it didn't take long for the investment terminology to drown me. "Basis points," "rebalancing," "short," "long," "index funds," "derivatives," "prospectus" – I quickly realized that this is why many people stay away from finance and why so many Americans aren't ready for retirement. Wall Street is too complicated, and if that's the case, then so is wealth. I didn't quit, though; a bit flustered, I decided to catch up. I bought book after book and slowly interviewed coworkers on the same floor until I met nearly everyone who worked in our division. I wanted to learn as much as I could and to demystify the world of Wall Street.

Before the conclusion of the internship, I accomplished my goal of demystifying Wall Street while uncovering a new one. I learned that I had been lied to, that the world of Wall Street thrives on your belief that you cannot invest on your own. I learned that building wealth can be simple and that, with all their financial calculations, there were thousands of average people without financial pedigree making more money than these high-end corporate experts.

From that point on, I became obsessed with discovering other lies that kept people from building wealth. Every day that summer, I read, I learned how to invest, and I learned how to start my own company. I created BuildingBread to teach people the truths about wealth, what it looks like, and how to obtain it. In addition to an information over-complication, there are three lies that we have learned to believe that keep us from learning how to properly build wealth.

I also learned that financial success does not always wear a suit or live in the big city. Wealth can be found anywhere, and there are multiple ways to achieve it. Wealth is available to those who welcome it and those whose mind is open to growth rather than consistent comfort. Anyone who tells you that money is only reserved for a certain population or profession is not only lying but likely does not have wealth themselves.

Whatever you think you know about money likely isn't true; you've been sold a bill of lies through popular television, magazines, conversations with friends, and even through school. We'll address each of these areas separately and dispel all of the lies you've been taught to believe and embrace as realistic and, worse, accepted as the common truth. Beware of these mindsets, for your mindset determines the direction of your money.

The "Reality" TV Lie

Reality television, in my estimation, has to be one of the most dangerous inventions in recent history. It was meant for entertainment, but over the past ten years, it has not only become the norm, but also a huge generator of our financial problems.

Let's take the definition of wealth. When looking at the average television program, who do you think or know to be wealthy? Nearly any Real Housewives show is bound to lead you on the wrong path. As I stated earlier, the number one occupation of millionaire housewives is school teacher. How often do you notice any of those women working on that show? How is it that, of all the strands of the show, not one of them has represented what a typical millionaire housewife is?

What's worse is the message that it sends not only to you, but to kids. What may seem like harmless entertainment is subliminally sending signals about what wealth is and what you are able to accomplish with it.

Wealth is not exclusively lavish. Wealth isn't always having a huge house and nice cars. Wealth is not about consumption, it's about conservation, and it's a lesson that is almost never taught on TV.

Remember that only 31 percent of parents consider themselves excellent role models when it comes to managing money and that kids learn most from the actions of their parents.

In that same study Capital One and ING found that 52 percent of kids reported learning their financial lessons from home, but home isn't the best place to learn that type of lesson – and that's coming from the parents!

The other 48 percent of kids are getting it from somewhere else, which ends up being primarily the small screen. Without their parents to redirect them toward reality, they grow up still living the lie and end up in the same financial places. I've seen it firsthand more times than I'd like to admit.

In the summer of 2012, I had the opportunity to train as a teacher in Houston, TX. As a fresh college grad, I tried my best to learn the ropes of an educator under the weight of the Texas heat. Before actually stepping into the classroom, we were granted the opportunity to meet the kids whom we were going to teach. At lunch, the once-empty, echoing cafeteria was slowly but steadily filling with sixth, seventh, and eighth graders. Being new, we were armed with a few questions to get the conversations started. "What's your favorite subject?" and, "What do you want to be when you grow up?" had become my main two weapons in disarming the awkward silence of a teacher sitting with you at lunch.

Though the interactions with the kids were refreshing, in the back of my head, I couldn't help but feel a bit depressed. All the boys wanted to be NFL players or MLS stars. As I continued to delve deeper into the motivations behind their proposed career choices, the answers only got worse. One student – let's call him Jason – wanted nothing more than to play in the NFL.

When asked why, he said he wanted to make money to take care of his family. He and I went back and forth, me asking him why and him explaining to me why his career choice was so perfect for his situation.

Why was this a depressing situation? Ask any middle-schooler, and his or her aspirations will revolve around professional athletics, right?

The truth is, that's not exactly the case. Among low-SES (socioeconomic status) schools, you'll find that more students are banking on athletics as their *only* way out of their current situation. I have noticed that this is more accentuated for African-American students. This is the case because, again – going back to television – the only millionaires they see come with a jersey of some type or a microphone. Their definition of wealth at that age will most likely come from two channels: BET and ESPN. This situation is particularly depressing because, without intervention, their aspirations may fade, but their definitions of wealth, how to obtain it, and how to build it will not.

There will come a time when age and physical ability will ultimately break the news to the majority of pro-athlete hopefuls, but what happens to them after this moment? Because they were only exposed to one way of seeing wealth and their opportunity was missed, it is highly unlikely that they will find another that will allow them to provide in the ways that they hoped.

Most people feel they cannot become what they cannot see. Again for African-Americans, this point is amplified. Images of wealthy individuals are rare, outside of athletes and entertainers, though there are a growing number to draw inspiration from. Seeing success matters.

In 1997, there were no South Korean golfers in the Ladies Professional Golf Association (LPGA) Tour, yet today there are more than forty; together, they win one third of all events. It was one person who sparked this surge, Se Ri Pak. In 1998, she won two major events[3], and it sent a wave of inspiration through South Korea.

When it comes to wealth in the majority of African-American communities, wealth building icons aren't usually the Ephern Taylors, Bob Johnsons or Reginald Lewises. They're Shawn "Jay-Z" Carter, Magic Johnson, and Oprah Winfrey, all very wealthy and respectable businessmen and –women. However, this sends the message that, to be wealthy, one must have a talent or be in front of the camera – which is not the case. Other cultures may be able to draw on the inspiration of a Bill Gates, Warren Buffett, or Mark Zuckerberg, in addition to athletes, showing a range of ways to become wealthy.

Daniel Coyle points to the "Windshield Effect." He argues in his book, *The Little Book of Talent*, that physically seeing an icon can ignite inspiration: "Studies show that even a brief connection with a role model can increase unconscious motivation." The African-American community is flooded with the images of athletes and entertainers, which, in turn, motivates more to pursue that route and subconsciously perpetuates that entertainment is the only way to build wealth if you're an African-American, which is far from the truth. In the broader American society, we have all been bombarded with incorrect images of what wealth is and how to obtain it.

This was the exact situation that was chronicled in ESPN's "30 for 30" documentary series, *Broke*. The documentary illustrates how multimillion dollar athletes made it to the top of their game on and off the court and managed to lose it all. Sports Illustrated noted that 78 percent of players in the NFL and 60 percent of players in the NBA are bankrupt 5 years

---

[3]   Coyle, D. (2012). The little book of talent: 52 tips for improving your skills. New York: Bantam Books.

after retiring. Perhaps some of the kids I met that day in Houston will go pro. I certainly will never be the teacher to stifle any kid's dream – as long as it isn't dangerous – but what's to stop them from repeating the same mistakes of athletes in the past if they get to that level?

When taking a look at those athletes who go broke, it would seem that they had lied to, and our kids have been lied to as well. How else could multi-millionaires lose all of their money so quickly? Clearly, they bought into a false projection of what wealth is and how the wealthy act.

Belief in the lie that lavish lifestyles are indications of wealth is the hardest to overcome. The athletes who fall into that trap are adults, some with families and many with college degrees. In the back of their minds, while they are receiving these monster paychecks, there is a voice that validates their outrageous spending habits: "This is what rich people do." "I earned this." "I can make this money back." "I'm supposed to spend my money."

These notions aren't specific to the multimillion dollar athletes; it's for the average person, as well. The true question is, where did these beliefs come from? How did we all learn that rich people live in large houses, that they have thirty- and forty-room mansions? Was it MTV's *Cribs*? Perhaps the movies? Regardless of where you learned it, the chance of your beliefs actually fading is slim to none. It's that reason that we're often shocked to learn that the majority of millionaires in the United States consist of not athletes, music stars or Wall Street CEOs, but business owners[4] – and not business owners in the traditional sense, either. Many of them, like Jeffery

---

[4]   Stanley, T. J. (2000). *The millionaire mind*. Kansas City: Andrews McMeel Pub.

Jones, own mobile home parks. Others are pest controllers, rice farmers, building contractors, and stamp and coin dealers.

Much different than you expected, isn't it? Knowing this, how many actual millionaires do you see on TV now? How many reality shows feature those who are actually *wealthy*? Could you imagine MTV shooting an episode of *Cribs* in Jeffery Jones' house? It might not be too exciting, but it would be the truth. And speaking of TV, the wealthy don't watch much of it. While the average American spends 34 hours each week watching TV millionaires are learning and earning[5]; millionaires average reading about two books per month usually on the topics of money management, history and biographies.

Today, the self-employed make up 20 percent of the workforce in the U.S., but they make up nearly 33 percent of all millionaires[6]. Even all the athletes, rappers, singers, talk show hosts, and actors combined still wouldn't make up the majority of the wealthy population. If you thought any differently, you've been lied to.

The Spending Lie

The Spending Lie is perhaps the most pervasive and persistent. It's the beliefs that you have to spend to display your income and status, or that those who may live a low-key lifestyle cannot possibly be rich.

---

[5] Hinckley, D. (2012, September 19). Americans spend 34 hours a week watching TV, according to Nielsen numbers . *NY Daily News.*

[6] Stanley, T. J. (2000). *The millionaire mind.* Kansas City: Andrews McMeel Pub.

It's the reason why we're shocked when a retired 80-year old teacher passes away and donates millions to a church. We wonder how a teacher who lived in the same house most of his life and drove an old Buick could ever save up that type of money.

The real question is, why should you have been shocked at all? Why do you continuously link riches with fancy cars and large houses? Maybe it's because you've been lied to. We have been raised to think that anyone who's rich has the following items: nice watches, cars, clothes, and homes. Not only is this not the case for the majority of the truly wealthy, it doesn't add up mathematically. Wealth is not about how much you spend, but *how much you have left*. The definition of wealth can be summed up in one question.

"If you were to stop getting paid today, but you still had to pay your bills, how much longer could you live like you are today?" This question addresses the exact definition of wealth and doesn't allow the person who is answering to make an easy assumption to feel better about him- or herself. A truly wealthy person will answer, "If I kept doing what I'm doing now? About 8 to 10 years, depending on how prices change."

Those who are wealthy do not depend on a paycheck to keep things going. If they lost their jobs in an instant, they would likely not panic. Not only have they saved their money, but they probably have one or two more ways to bring money in.

Ask someone who has been living The Spending Lie and they'll probably tell you this, "If I *didn't* pay bills, probably a week or so." Those who are not wealthy live paycheck to paycheck, regardless of how large that check is. So, how many fall into this category? The American Payroll Association on

Sep. 19, 2012, found that 68 percent of Americans would "find it difficult if their paychecks were delayed a week." [7] Whether you're making $100 a week or $1000, missing a paycheck can be painful if you're living The Spending Lie.

Living paycheck to paycheck doesn't necessarily mean you're not making enough money; it means you're spending too much. Maybe you're spending too much on your apartment just to have the location and recognition. Maybe your shoe addiction is too strong. The most common personal finance rule is, "Live below your means." Just because your paycheck reads $1500 does not and should not mean that you have exactly $1500 to spend. You are to live *below* your means, not live *at* your means. A $1500 paycheck should mean you have about $1320 to spend, including bills, because you took a portion of that check and paid yourself first.

By doing so, missing a paycheck won't ruin your finances. It's a simple rule, but 68 percent of people don't follow it, because The Spending Lie is so pertinent. When I lecture about the importance of saving and paying yourself first, the first reaction I always hear is, "I can't afford to do that; I don't have any money left." Again, you see how this Lie has led us into mismanaging money subliminally.

First, if this was your reaction, too, you're not alone. Second, you didn't follow the rule. Pay yourself *first*. There should be plenty left, because you haven't and shouldn't have paid anyone or anything until after you've received a cut (well, other than taxes). If saving money doesn't leave you enough to take care of the bills, then you need to stop buying into The Spending Lie and change your lifestyle until you have a

---

[7]   Majority of Americans Live Paycheck to Paycheck, Confident in Paycheck. (2012, September 17).

paycheck to match. You can't have a Wal-Mart salary and live in a corporate condo overlooking the skyline. That's not within your means yet, and you're doing something intended or serving to convey a false impression (ahem … a Lie).

What exactly does living beneath your means look like, and how do you do it? Let's look to a senior citizen from Omaha, Nebraska; we'll call him Mr. B. In 1958, he bought his first house for $31,500, where he still lives today. Currently, Mr. B is 83 years young, carries no cell phone, does not have a computer at his desk at work, and loves to eat at Dairy Queen. To get to and from work, as well as complete his errands, Mr. B drives his Cadillac DTS.

Does it sound like Mr. B lives paycheck to paycheck or lives The Spending Lie? Does Mr. B live beneath his means? The answers may shock you. Mr. B is none other than Warren Buffet, the second richest man in the United States and ranked as the fifteenth most powerful person in the country. Yes, you heard right.

The second richest man in the country not only is an 83-year-old man who drives a Cadillac but also still lives in the house he bought before he became super wealthy. Buffett is worth $58 billion; with that type of wealth, I'm more than certain that he could afford a mansion, eat at better places than Dairy Queen, and at least hire a full-time driver to chauffer him around Omaha.

However, Warren Buffet has decided not to, because he does not believe in The Spending Lie. Just because he is a billionaire does not mean he has to spend his money like one. No private jets, no 24-inch rims, no BMW, and certainly not a Maybach! Those who believe in he Spending Lie will tout these items as if it makes them richer than those around them, when, in reality, it shows how obviously poor they really are. It shows where their priorities are and where their money isn't.

The Spending Lie doesn't affect just the super-rich; it also hurts those who are currently struggling. The Spending Lie is the reason a man will own a car with rims and a speaker system worth more than the car itself but doesn't own a house. It's the reason why hundreds of people will line up at Footlocker to buy shoes upwards of $150. Millionaires and billionaires whose wealth lasts don't do that. If billionaire Warren Buffett drives a discreet, non-tricked-out Cadillac, why do people with much less think it's more than okay to drive a $250,000 Maybach? Buffett's house wasn't even worth that when he bought it in 1958. Living well beyond your means doesn't show that you're rich; it proves that you're stupid.

Perhaps author Dennis Kimbro captured it best: "The poor keep score by cars and clothes; the middle class keep score by degrees and titles; but the wealthy keep score by their bank account."

The Paycheck Lie

Another common financial Lie that persists in our lives is The Paycheck Lie. It's the belief that, "As long as I have a good job, I can afford to pay these bills." This is a very dangerous lifestyle and is another reason why too many Americans live paycheck to paycheck. Remember that the definition of wealth is how much money you have left –in other words, it's how much of your paycheck you have left. The more you have sitting around, the wealthier you are.

Because the majority of people believe The Paycheck Lie, it leads us to break the golden rule of finance (live beneath your means.) Subscribers to the Lie contend that, as long as the bills are getting paid, things are okay. But here's the catch: if you miss a paycheck, what happens? And worse, what happens when you're too old to work? You certainly don't want to be 65 or 70 and forced to work just to keep the lights on. Sure, you're able to pay the bills now, but you won't be able to do it forever.

We often believe in the "earn more, spend more" axiom. If we want to spend more, we need to work more … but why are we trying to spend so much to begin with?

The Paycheck Lie, unlike the others, can also take on another form. It sounds like this: "I need to make a million dollars or more per year; only those making that much are wealthy." The average income in the U.S. is around $50,000.

That being the fact, every millionaire and billionaire in the country should be making a bare minimum of $1 million, right?

This is yet another complete and utter lie. Most millionaires have an income of $131,000[8]. The percentage of millionaires that make $1 million or more per year is 5 percent, and those who make $500,000 to $999,999 is 8 percent. You don't have to make a million to be a millionaire.

Well, what about the rest of us? Does that mean you can never be wealthy? The answer is no – you can absolutely be wealthy (if not, I wouldn't have written this book.) If you want to become wealthy – you must learn some of the lessons of the wealthy. We'll get more into it later, but there is one thing very important to note.

Becoming wealthy has much less to do about your income than it does about how you manage it. Remember, you don't

---

[8] Stanley, T. J. (2000). *The millionaire mind*. Kansas City: Andrews McMeel Pub.

have to make a million to be a millionaire; only 5 percent of millionaires do that. Instead, you need to invest more of your time in managing what you have rather than trying solely to make more of it.

In Chapter 4: The Blueprint we'll get more into specifics on how to become wealthy with what you have now, as well as what your wealth goal should be.

The final piece of The Paycheck Lie is that income equals wealth. That isn't the case at all. Let's look at Mr. Diggs, CEO of a top Wall Street firm in New York City. Diggs has a corner office, wears only designer suits, and has a driver take him to and from work.

On the weekends, Mr. Diggs enjoys working from his favorite residence, a midtown condo that overlooks Manhattan. As a CEO, Mr. Diggs has a top-rate corporate salary; he is paid $3.7 million per year.

It is no doubt that Mr. Diggs has a very large paycheck. But, is he a millionaire? Let's find out. Mr. Diggs owns a total of three residences, costing him a total of $25 million. He spends about $3 million per year on himself alone, not including his children's private school, his wife, who has an infamous shopping habit, and their vacations.

Mr. Diggs, on average, spends about $4 million per year, yet he only makes $3.7 million. He has no savings, because he feels he can get by on his current paycheck and expects to get paid more.

The truth is, Mr. Diggs is far from rich. He's in debt, because he spends more than he actually makes. He is not a millionaire; he's broke. Mr. Diggs, despite all of the things he has, is living The Spending Lie and lives paycheck to paycheck. Mr. Diggs could not even last a year without receiving a paycheck.

The fact is, Mr. Diggs is actively living The Paycheck Lie. He makes just enough to pay the bills and uses credit cards to cover the excess. He does all of this just because he can but would be very, very worried if the company were to fail or his pay were to be cut.

Mr. Diggs has a younger sister by the name of Michelle Collins. The two grew up in rural Kansas, but as her brother branched off for college and Wall Street, Michelle stayed close to home. She married soon after college and now teaches kindergarten. Her husband owns a local dry-cleaning business. The two combined have an income of $95,000. They own one house and have two kids who both attend public school. Both drive older, used cars. On average, Michelle and her husband spend about $65,000 per year.

Though her brother makes almost 40 times more money than her and her husband combined, she is much more wealthy than he is. First, because she has $30,000 left over each year to save or invest. They live beneath their means; they are not worried if the business fails, because they have savings to fall back on until they can find another way. If neither of them got paid next year, they would be able to survive nearly six months. That's much longer than what her executive brother can say. Currently, neither is a millionaire, but it's obvious who is on their way.

This isn't an aberration; it's the norm. Those making high incomes, such as CEOs, entertainers, and athletes, are not exempt from the laws of basic math. Don't spend more than what you bring in. Whether your paycheck is big or small, The Paycheck Lie will leave you in a rat race of working and praying that your check is never late. That's not wealth, and it certainly isn't the way money should work.

I think now you can see how and why these lies can cripple your finances. Most notably, these lies hit lotto winners the hardest. While many believe that money changes you, I contend that money enhances who you already are.

The only things that change are your ability to afford whatever demons you may have already had harboring inside you. For lottery winners and anyone expecting a large sum of cash, you should be especially careful.

The Paycheck Lie can be best observed from the scores of fallen lottery winners all across the country. Canadian Gerald Muswagon won $10 million in the Super 7 jackpot in 1998. Within seven years, he had spent it all partying and drinking. William Post, after winning more than $16 million in Pennsylvania, ended up with $1 million in debt and lives off of food stamps.

Evelyn Adams, perhaps the most interesting lottery winner, won not once, but twice, in both 1985 and 1986. She gambled a grand total of $5.4 million away. This shouldn't be a shock, since money enhances who you already are[9] – after all, buying lottery tickets is a form of gambling.

These examples are not outliers. A quick Google search will show you hundreds of men and women who squandered a fortune, often in less than five years. All of these winners fell for The Paycheck Lie. They spent above and beyond their enormous means and ended up back where they started – and, for some, worse off than where they began.

Expecting a large amount of money, whether it's from a lotto ticket, graduation, or a holiday bonus, can damage your finances

---

[9]   Doll, J. (2012, March 30). A Treasury of Terribly Sad Stories of Lotto Winners. *The Wire.*

if you don't pay attention. According to Jason Zweig, author of *Your Money and Your Brain*, when grocery shoppers come across instant coupons in the store, they spend nearly 12 percent more on sporadic purchases than other shoppers. It affects more than shoppers, too. In 2001, every U.S. taxpayer received a rebate of up to $600 as a part of President Bush's tax reform. Those who felt the rebate was extra money (as opposed to getting their own money back) spent three times more[10].

The amount of money that you expect doesn't change your behavior. Zweig reports in an experiment that one group of college students was told they would get to spend $5 the next day at a basketball game; a second group showed up at the game and was handed $5 without warning. The students who got the surprise money spent more than twice as much as those who knew it was coming.

Winning or finding unexpected money can cause you to spend more than you intended. Perhaps this was the case with many lottery winners, but the Lies still come into play, and again, by simply following the golden rule of personal finance, these disasters can be avoided, no matter how much money you come across.

The Greed Lie

Last of the four financial lies is The Greed Lie. Not every wealthy person is a saint; it would be asinine to believe that. If it were true, that would mean that everyone in the middle class is perfect and has the absolute best moral background. You and I both know that that's a lie. No population of people

---

[10] Zweig, J. (2007). Your money and your brain: how the new science of neuroeconomics can help make you rich. New York: Simon & Schuster.

can be generalized and stereotyped, nor should they be. Trends in the news and politics have done a great job of portraying all those who are wealthy as men and women with cold hearts and no morals.

The Greed Lie is the subscription to the belief that, to become wealthy, you have to cheat someone to get to the top. Subsequently, this Lie makes it more comfortable for those who do not achieve financial success to be more comfortable with their own mediocrity. The people quickest to discount the importance of financial independence are usually those deepest in debt.

In addition, it's a commonly held belief that being wealthy comes with a lot of stress. That may be true, but it is certainly stressful for people who don't have a roof over their heads, as well. In fact, those making $10,000 per year are 50 percent times more likely to commit suicide than people making $60,000[11].

Perhaps most convincing for some was an article published by Caroline Fairchild in 2012 whose title read, "Suicide rates higher for Americans living among wealthy neighborhoods." Just reading the title may reaffirm your beliefs and misconceptions, but upon further research, you will notice something very interesting about these findings. The title reads "*Americans living among*" wealthy neighborhoods, **not** the wealthy themselves.

Living beyond your means can produce much more stress than you think. This is another example of The Spending Lie and not living within your own financial limitations.

---

[11]   Fairchild, C. (2012, November 9). Suicide Rates Higher For Americans Living Among Wealthy Neighbors: Study. *The Huffington Post.*

In the same year Fairchild published her article, *Business Insider* released its findings on a San Francisco Federal Reserve study on the same topic: "While the effect was seen among high-earning individuals, the most vulnerable to this phenomenon are low-income people living amongst the wealthy."[12] The lesson: it's called personal finance for a reason – because it's *personal*. Trying to outspend and constantly comparing yourself to others will not make you rich; in fact, it could have an opposite effect, much worse than going broke.

Creating wealth for yourself takes time, patience, and modesty. We've learned through The Spending Lie that many of America's wealthy are not the flashy ones we see on TV. They're more likely to drive a Mazda than a Mercedes and look more like your average Sunday school teachers than the couple showing off their shopping bags at the mall.

You'll learn much more about what the wealthy actually do and what they look like in the next section, but for now, stop and think about everything you think you know about the rich and try to trace it back to the source.

Was it the coverage of people like Bernie Maddoff? Was it Donald Trump's reality show, *The Apprentice*? Or maybe it was the select few kids on MTV's Sweet 16? As you can see, each of the examples above represents one of the lies you've likely been fed about money. Whether or not you watched these shows with regularity, you've likely heard about them. As a recent college grad, I often overheard conversations about how people planned to spend their refund check before they had even received a dime. Rarely did those conversations mention saving a portion or buying stocks. The Reality TV,

---

[12]   Woodruff, M. (2012, November 12). 'Keeping Up With The Joneses' Could Lead To Suicide. *Business Insider*.

Spending, Paycheck and Greed Lies run deep in our psyche. And if laying out each lie isn't convincing enough, maybe spelling out the truth will be more convincing. After all, the truth shall set you free.

Conclusion

I started college in late August 2008, my parents and I had driven 21 hours from Tulsa, Oklahoma to Hampton, Virginia and it wasn't until they drove away that I had noticed I didn't bring a TV. With no car, it wouldn't be the feasible to just buy a new one. But, as many college students handle pressing issues, I ignored it. By default, I ended up reading more and I haven't owned a TV with cable since – and I do not plan to do so anytime soon. It wasn't until I turned off the TV that I began to read books like the *Automatic Millionaire* and *Think and Grow Rich*.

This is what launched me, not only in my career as a wealth coach, but also into changing my mindset about building wealth. My dad had taught me all the skills, but I was just going through the motions. We're all guilty, at times of not following good advice, and it's usually because we're distracted or just plain stubborn. Don't be distracted by financial lies and lifestyles.

Thinking the way the majority of people do will get you where the majority of people are: not so financially savvy, concerned about their job security and your next paycheck. You now have a choice to continue to subscribe, believe, and act the way wealthy people do or you can stay on course with those who struggle. The road to wealth, as well as success, will always begin in your mind. When you change your mind, you can change your actions. Without changing something within yourself, no roadmap or budgeting technique will make you wealthy.

Wealth begins first in the mind, not through affirmations and quotations, but in how you think. How determined you are and how focused your goals are will determine how far you will go. I often harken back to a story my management professor liked to tell: he said that there was a guy who was once famous on Wall Street. Due to the economy, he was out on the streets before he could blink; he had lost everything. When he was on top of the world, he would smoke a cigar from a secret drawer in his desk. Even as a homeless man, he could never kick the habit. He knew that each cigar smoked left one butt. If he could find five cigar butts, he could make one full cigar. "Well, one day he found 25 cigar butts. How many cigars did he make?"

You, like the rest of my classmates and myself probably jumped to the quick answer: 5. We were all wrong; the correct answer was 6. Initially he could make five cigars each, which would have left one butt apiece – allowing him to make one extra cigar. How you think will determine if you will build wealth. The situation you may be born into may not be perfect; the cards you are dealt do not have to be perfect. Life is about overcoming adversity. Life is about playing a bad hand of cards well.

You have a choice. Believe and resolve in your mind now that you can build wealth, no matter where you are, or listen to the nine poor people around you, and wait to become the tenth.

CHAPTER TWO

The Truth About Wealth

The truth is that the picture that you have of wealthy people is probably way off. It's most likely the difference between the hustle and bustle of New York City and the small town life of Cushing, Oklahoma (feel free to look that up.)

In this section, I'm going to lay out all of the traits and descriptors of the wealthy in America – the truly wealthy, not those who have huge salaries with debt to match, nor those who are rich now but likely to be poor later.

You'll find almost no athletes, actors, or musicians in any of these findings, because most (not all) fall prey to the Spending and Paycheck Lie, and both will leave you broke sooner or later.

Most people believe that, to get rich, you have to get lucky. For some, their wealth plan is to win the lottery or marry into a rich family. Others believe that the majority of today's wealthy have become rich through old money or inheritance.

The truth is, most American millionaires are first-generation rich. This has almost always been the case. According to Dr.

Stanley, in 1892, a man by the name of Stanley Lebergott concluded that 84% of the then 4,047 millionaires were "nouveau riche, having reached the top without the benefit of inherited wealth."[13]

More truths about the rich having money:

- 91% have never received, as a gift, as much as $1 of the ownership of a family business
- Nearly half never received any college tuition from their parents or other relatives
- Only 2% of millionaires inherited any part of their homes and property

Earlier, we discussed the Spending and Paycheck Lies; let's look at those in reference to America's wealthy. Recall that most millionaires have an income of $131,000. With that type of money, they could afford to wear and ride in almost anything you can imagine. But despite that type of paycheck, those who have true wealth may shock you with their spending habits.

Let's take shoes. Personally, I find it fascinating that hundreds of people line up to fork over hundreds of dollars for a pair of shoes. For the price of a plane ticket, these people will wait in lines to buy something that won't make them walk on water, or even want to walk in the rain for that matter. Appearance is important, but how many business deals are you going to score in a pair of Jordan's? Exactly. The cost to make J's is less than $10, but people are more than willing to pay $150, $200, or even $300 to get their feet in them. Naturally, with a $131,000-a-year income, those who are wealthy can have

---

[13] Stanley, T. J., & Danko, W. D. (1996). *The millionaire next door: the surprising secrets of America's wealthy*. Atlanta, Ga.: Longstreet Press.

more than a few pairs of these exclusive kicks, if not some shoes that are even more expensive.

I would say that I hate to break it to you, but I don't. Half of millionaires in the U.S. have never paid more than $140 for a pair of shoes, and three out of four have never paid more than $199. The sad truth is that the ones who can most afford those shoes are relaxing, while those who struggle to put gas in their car are scraping to buy shoes that they won't wear more than a few times a month.

When it comes to watches, the wealthy still have about the same spending threshold. Half of all millionaires have never spent more than $235 for a watch. The average millionaire in this country has a net worth (the amount of money they have left after the bills have been paid in full) of $9.2 million. Yet, more than half have never spent more than $200 for shoes. If millionaires don't pay that much for accessories, then why are you so eager to have them? You undoubtedly have a friend or two – or maybe this is you we're talking about – who boasts a collection of "fly kicks" and one or two very expensive watches. And you and I both know that your friend's net worth is a lot less than $9 million.

One rule of thumb to go by: if he looks "rich," he probably isn't. The typical rich person, if you're still clinging to those lies, probably drives a nice BMW or a Jag, right? By now, you've caught onto the trend that they probably do not ride around in limos and own Aston Martins and Bentleys. It would make sense that many of the rich and powerful would drive a BMW. It's cheap enough, in comparison to a Bentley, and anyone making a decent pay should be able to afford one. It's the perfect car that says, "I've earned this," without being in-your-face, like a Lamborghini would. If these were your thoughts, I'm glad you've scaled down your bias a bit, but you're still a long way off.

The number one car brand bought by millionaires is a Ford – the most popular model being the Ford F-150![14]

Half of all millionaires have never spent more than $30,000 on a car, which eliminates many common luxury car brands. Cadillac and Lincoln come in second and third, respectively. With that much wealth, surely these millionaires could afford something more fitting for someone with $9 million, right? But what would be the point in doing so? No one gets paid for proving his or her wealth –though one can certainly lose it that way.

Okay, so they don't drive the nicest cars or wear the flashiest clothes. At least you'll be able to spot their house on the corner. Perhaps then you can walk up, knock on the door, and ask them for their financial wisdom. Well, let's think about it first. If you have $2 million, you're not going to live in a $2 million house. Why would you? That would mean that you would have nothing left with which to pay the bills or fill the fridge; let's not even mention furnishing a $2 million home! You'd be living right *at* your means, which isn't a good thing.

Only 25% of millionaires have buy a house costing $1 million or more; most of them bought their house for $435,000. Note, though, that these are millionaires who make, on average, $131,000 a year. Yet, because of the Spending and Paycheck Lie, 30% of people making just $60,000 or less live in homes worth $300,000. It's no wonder that the housing market crashed in 2008. 30% of Americans were living in homes *intended or serving to convey a false impression of wealth.*

---

[14] Stanley, T. J., & Danko, W. D. (1996). *The millionaire next door: the surprising secrets of America's wealthy.* Atlanta, Ga.: Longstreet Press.

Who Are These People?!

We've learned that the vast majority of truly wealthy individuals are not flashy but conservative in their spending. But to save hundreds of thousands – even millions – has to be stressful, right? Those who become millionaires have to be greedy, old misers and penny-pinchers who would put Scrooge to shame. We know what they drive and what they don't wear, but what *do* these people look like, and what do they value? How can you model your actions to become one of the wealthy?

Dr. Stanley perhaps paints the best picture of the wealthy in his two books, *The Millionaire Mind* and *The Millionaire Next Door*. Here are his findings on who the wealthy really are:

- The typical millionaire is 54 and has been married to the same woman for 28 years. One in four has been married to the same spouse for 38 years or more.
- Millionaires have 3 children, on average.
- 92% are married, only 2% have never been married.
- Many have never spent more than $1,500 for an engagement ring.
- 50% of their wives do not work outside the home.
- 10% are lawyers, and 9% are doctors.
- 32% are entrepreneurs, and 16% corporate executives.
- The other third is comprised of retired teachers, middle managers, accountants, sales professionals, engineers, professors, and homemaker

Perhaps this is not the picture you were envisioning, especially when it comes to marriage. It has become an extremely popular notion that marriage is overrated and that financial success can probably be achieved without a partnership.

Popular media would also have you thinking that the divorce rate is much higher among the wealthy or that, to stay wealthy, you'd have to live a lonely life devoid of family and friends.

This is not the case. Millionaires are often average-looking people with extraordinary planning and budgeting skills – two skills that you can learn.

Notice, too, that attorneys and doctors, two professions known for creating very high incomes, do not make up a huge percentage of the wealthy. Though you can become wealthy in those professions, it would seem that the key is self-employment or entrepreneurship.

It's also important to note that teachers and middle managers, who are known to generate average incomes, are also capable of creating wealth. The management of your money is worth more than the money itself.

Now that we know what wealth looks like, let's find out more about what wealthy people believe. What are their values? Does money drive them? And what do they feel is the key to financial success? Again, Dr. Stanley sums it up best. In his study, he surveyed hundreds of millionaires nationwide and asked them what made them successful. What factors went into building their wealth?

There were more than 30 factors they felt helped them become successful. The top five are as follows:

1 Integrity
2 Discipline/self-control
3 Social skills
4 A supportive spouse
5 Hard work (working harder than most others)

Notice that luck, greed, or penny-pinching weren't big factors in generating wealth. In fact, the number one value, as told by millionaires, is the exact opposite of greed. Integrity, or being honest even when no one is looking, was the biggest factor in creating and retaining wealth. Next are discipline and self-control. In Stanley's research, these were actually tied for first. It will be nearly impossible to create and keep a fortune if you lack discipline and self-control.

Without it, you will never create a budget, let alone stick to it. You'll never be able to resist impulse-buying or the temptation to overspend. It takes a great deal of self-control to become wealthy. Fortunately, if you feel that you are lacking in that department, there are ways you can build it up and I'll show you how in Chapter 6.

Social skills makes it into the top five, dispelling the myth that the wealthy are lonely people who spend their lives counting their cash rather than counting their blessings. Spending time with friends and family ranks very high on the wealthy's keys to success. After all, it is very hard to build wealth alone. If you are an entrepreneur, you will need to persuade customers and, as a corporate executive, you will need superior social skills to lead your employees or to close a big business deal. Very rarely can someone be successful in a vacuum. Along with social skills, a supportive spouse is a key factor in success. Again, it's often too hard to do it alone, and there can be nothing more inspiring and driving than the person you love most becoming your biggest cheerleader.

Last, but certainly not least, rounding out the top five key factors in becoming financially successful is hard work. If you want to make it to the top of any field, hard work is required. It won't always be easy to become wealthy – if it were, everyone would have already done it! *You will have to be willing to do what many won't to get what many don't.*

So, where do all those other traits, like luck, rank in creating financial success? Millionaires said luck ranks 27th in the list of factors most important to building wealth. And surprisingly, graduating at or near the top of the class ranks dead last, at 30th. Though school is important (80% of millionaires are college grads), many of the financial elite weren't superstar students, with an average undergraduate GPA of 2.92 and SAT score of 1190.[15] Even graduating from a so-called "selective" or "prestigious" college or university doesn't rank very high on their list.

Building wealth depends much more on your *personal integrity, discipline, social skills, your spouse, and work ethic* than your college GPA and what school you came from, according to the millionaires themselves.

Lastly, as we depart from the topic describing what and whom America's wealthy really are, it's important to know what they do with their time. In addition to their most important values and their spending habits (recall the Ford F-150), you need to know what they do during the year, so that you may do the same as you design your fortune. Over the course of one year, more than 700 wealthy men and women were asked to carry a journal. During that year, over 85% visited with a tax expert, 81% had been to a museum, 68% participated in community activities, 67% gardened, and 64% raised money for charities.

While these findings may not be exciting, notice what was not on the list that you may often assume the wealthy spend their

---

[15] Stanley, T. J. (2000). *The millionaire mind.* Kansas City: Andrews McMeel Pub.

time doing: vacationing in the mountains, a safari in South Africa, and deep sea diving aren't activities that many of them do. In fact, only 4% report having skied in the Alps within the past year.

Now, you have a complete picture of what wealth actually looks like and what skills you will need to have to begin building it on your own. Next, we'll go into what happens if you ignore the most basic personal finance rules and you stretch your paycheck out too far. But, before we go to that, I want you to pause and reflect on these questions:

What have you learned about millionaires that has shocked you the most? Why was this surprising news?

Before reading this section, what did you think were the most important keys to building wealth?

Of the Five Factors, which was the most shocking to you?

Now that you know what those with true wealth have (and don't have), what are some areas in which you've overspent?

Going back to the Lies about money, which Lie affected you the most?

You have just seen a picture of true wealth – not through television or hearsay, but through research. And the research says that you, too, can build your own wealth, if you follow the same path: common-sense spending and saving. It may not be the fastest route in the world, but you have to think…would you rather get rich quickly or stay rich slowly? Now that you know how most people fail financially and what success looks like, it is time to learn how to create it for yourself.

For the dedicated, the passionate, and the confident, wealth will be yours to have, enjoy, and pass on within the following pages of this book. Many will hold the blueprints to achievement, but 80 percent will not have the confidence to believe that they can actually pull it off. You will also need to have the dedication to be consistent enough to save their money or press on through adversity. Because of this, they'll feel that financial success has always eluded them when, in reality, it was there all along. Now that you've made it this far, it is time to show you how to build solid wealth.

CHAPTER THREE

How to Defeat Your Debt

Debt will be absolutely unavoidable if you decide to live a lifestyle that is more lavish than today's millionaires without their type of money. It's like having champagne tastes with beer money: it just isn't going to happen.

If you want to live the life of a millionaire, you're going to have to work for it and not take the shortcut of plastic and payments. In this chapter, we'll get into the dangers of debt, the difference between good and bad debt, how to avoid it, when to use it, and why it's so damn easy to fall into it.

When you owe someone, you're in debt. If you spend more than you actually have, you're in debt. Each time you swipe your credit card, you are creating debt. Anytime you're in debt, you don't really have anything – but you can end up owing everything. And, more importantly, anytime you're in debt, you are making someone else rich.

Debt comes in two forms: revolving credit and installment debt. Generally, installment debt can be considered "good debt." These are loans that have to be paid back in separate but equal amounts and have a clear end date.

A mortgage is an installment debt, as are student loans, because mortgages are usually paid off in 30 years, student loans in 10 years. Each of these could be considered investments, as well – certainly your education. A *reasonable* amount of installment debt is okay to have.

When it comes to student loans, you have to be especially careful. Yes, taking out debt for college can be an investment, but it really depends on your field of study and what you do while you are in college. For parents with college-age children, it is very important to stress financial aid, degree options, and internships (preferably paid internships) while attending school. As a parent, you may have to take out loans for your child or co-sign on loans in case your child does not finish or has no job after graduation. This would leave you with additional debt. In 2011, the U.S. Bureau of Labor Statistics reported that 12.8 million young people under the age of 30 are either unemployed or underemployed (working in jobs that don't require a college degree.)[16]

When taking on large debt, you must have a plan to tackle it, before it tackles you. Not having a plan to pay off your debt is a de facto plan for financial disaster. Many people struggle with student loans because they are not organized, the debt is often in large amounts and you're not sure what loan to focus your attention on.

A quick fix to these problems is to list all of your debts in order of their amounts. Though financial academics often debate this method, it's best to focus most of your attention on the smallest amount (while paying small amounts to all the

---

[16] Fairbanks, A. (2011, April 22). Recent Graduates Not Only Move Back Home, But Stay There. *The Huffington Post.*

other loans) until it is paid off and move to the next. It is called the Snowball Method.

Those who majored in finance will argue that, due to interest rates, this isn't the best way to eliminate debt; however, finance does not account for psychology and human behavior. When you completely pay off smaller debts, you gain a psychological boost that further motivates you to continue eliminating your debts. As financial knowledge guru Dave Ramsey states, personal finance is 20 percent finance and 80 percent behavior. I was a first generation college student when I attended Hampton University. Having received zero dollars in scholarship money, the majority of my financial aid was grants and loans --mostly the latter. I graduated with five digits' worth of student debt, but I also graduated with a plan that made my payoff stress-free. The majority of stress, especially financial stress, comes from the lack of planning, not necessarily a lack of funds.

All debt can be dangerous, if not used properly. But the most dangerous debt at any given time is revolving credit, also known as consumer debt. This comes mainly from credit cards. The reason that they're so dangerous is that credit card debt has the ability to grow and never get paid off. Those that live the Paycheck and Spending Lies are the ones who are most likely to be in serious debt. Credit cards allow you to live above your means; they're small loans that you owe the credit card companies. The more you swipe, the more you have to pay them, and because of interest rates, you will always owe the credit card companies more than what a purchased item actually cost.

For example, imagine that you're hosting a Super Bowl party for your friends. Because everyone is coming to your house for the big game, you decide to head to the grocery store to stock up. You want to impress and show your friends a good time. When you get to the checkout, the total is $200. You know you don't have $200 to spend at the moment. But because everyone else is in line preparing for the big game, you don't want to embarrass yourself by asking the cashier to take several of the items off to lower the price. You begin to check around to see if anyone is looking as the impatient cashier holds her hand out for payment.

To defuse the situation, you whip out your credit card, key in your zip code, and quickly head to the car. "Perfect, I get to have my party and I don't have to pay that $200 until next month," you think. But next month comes, and you still don't have the $200. So, you decide to pay the minimum payment of $20 instead. This process continues, and you've come to realize that, in April, you've paid $240 for what originally cost you $200.

Moral of the story? Credit cards can be very deceiving. They make you think that, just because you can afford a small, $20 minimum payment, you can get those shoes you bought or the latest edition of Madden that you swiped for. Just because you can pay the monthly bill doesn't mean you can afford it or should own it. Why pay $100 for something that only cost $50 to begin with?

Americans seem to have a hard time with credit card debt. As of 2012, each household has an average of $15,956 in credit card debt. That type of money could buy a brand new car! That amount suggests that the average American household is living above their means by almost $16,000. The Paycheck Lie will tell you that $16,000 is not a lot of money; it's just $667 a month for two years. You can afford that.

The truth is that you may never pay that off. To eliminate such a large debt, not only would you have to pay large amounts every month, you would also have to not swipe your card for the next two years – not even once; otherwise, the amount would grow even larger.

You'll likely never swipe a credit card for a single $16,000 purchase, but you will swipe for furniture, the flat-screen TV you saw on sale on Black Friday, and a few outfits. All of those items add up, and if you never pay the smaller items off, that credit card bill will get higher and higher. The question becomes this: why do we feel the need to buy these things when we know we don't have the money? Essentially, that's what credit cards allow us to do. When you don't have the money, your credit card says, "Don't worry, I've got you. You can just pay me back later."

The answer is this: We feel much more of a need to convey a false impression than to become financially independent, and the things that make an impression can be seen. Cars, clothes, and flat screen TVs can be great conversation starters and garner a lot of attention. When you can impress people like that, it can be fun and exciting.

Being financially independent has an inward focus. You won't be flaunting your bank account to people. You won't be stressed about your paycheck being a day late. You're responsible, patient, and smart with your money, and none of those attributes can be explicitly shown to impress people.

All financial advice can come down to that principle. Are you trying to impress or be independent? From the car lot to the fitting room, imagine what would happen if everyone thought about this principle. I'd imagine that Nike would lose a lot of business. The hundreds of people who sleep outside the store to buy shoes are trying to impress. Those whose music can be heard from blocks away before they can be seen are trying to impress, and it is likely that neither of these types of people are financially independent.

It will be much easier to build wealth when you aren't weighed down by credit card debt. Debt is the exact opposite of wealth. You can have all the things you *think* the wealthy have, with all of the stress and worries that they don't. Recall from the earlier chapters that those who are already wealthy aren't too concerned with showing off their money. The children of most millionaires don't even realize that their parents are rich until they are adults and have kids of their own. If you want to be financially independent, you have to stop lying to yourself and stop trying to impress others.

Additionally, when it comes to debt, you have the ability to negotiate on your behalf. Though debt collectors can seem intimidating, they need you on board, and they are often willing to agree to a payment plan. Even with credit cards, you are always able to negotiate your interest rate and pay-off schedule. The key being unafraid to ask.

This is something that you can handle on your own. Some debt counseling services will charge you a fee for doing exactly what you can do yourself. By listing out your debts and revealing to a creditor your own personal payment timeline and committing to that timeline; you can save time, money and stress. You should also keep a written record of whom you speak with and the time and the date of all interactions. Documenting these communications with creditors is important; it shows them that you are serious about repaying your debt, and it also allows you to relate any necessary details if you are routed to a different person. If at all possible, it is best to talk with the same person at all times so that you know they are familiar with you and your situation.

Avoiding Debt

Of course, instead of ending up in debt you could always avoid it altogether. To do so you need to get into the habit of saving early and often, both for big project such as college or smaller things like a new TV. Waiting and saving isn't always the fun thing to do but I can guarantee it is more fun than having to pay down a bill every month.

One reason why using credit is so attractive is because it breaks large purchases into smaller amounts. A $50,000 car is just $700 per month, a new laptop just $150 per month. These amounts are pretty affordable, but instead of paying it to a credit card company or pawn shop why not pay it to yourself and save money on the interest?

While my fiancée was in graduate school someone stole her 13 inch MacBook Pro and her cell phone. The phone was found using an app she downloaded the computer was not, leaving her with not only lost memories and music but without the ability to continue her studies in the way she was used to. Her only income was her work-study job restricting her to no more than 20 hours per week at about $9 per hour. She needed a computer fast.

Perhaps the simple quick solution would have been going to the nearest electronic store to finance a new $1200 MacBook. Had she done so, she could have made payments of $80 or so per month for 18 months. However, this would have cost her $1,440; over $200 more than what the laptop actually costs. Instead I decided to pay for the laptop as a birthday gift out of my savings and pay myself an extra $100 per month for one year.

There was no point in paying extra money in interest charges when you can simply make payments to yourself instead. Just because you can afford the monthly payment doesn't mean that it is something that you should do. Be patient and make payments to yourself instead of taking out a loan or using your credit card. By taking the time and making payments to yourself, you are actually doing yourself a bigger favor than you realize. Realistically speaking depending on the type of item you are buying, it is going to take time to save up enough money to buy it in cash. Even if you buy using a loan or a credit card it will still take a while to pay the bill completely off. When you go into debt for an item you get that item right then, but when you save for it you have to wait until you have the full amount. Fortunately for the saver, good things come to those who wait. Cars and electronics, like most items improve as time goes on. Buying on credit allows you to continue to pay for an item that continues to become obsolete while waiting and saving will allow you to buy the best product without continuing to pay for it after a better product comes.

Conclusion

If you want to build wealth, you must actively attack your existing debt and avoid the temptation to create new debt. Sometimes, that means waiting to buy certain things; it could mean sending your kids to a community college before going to a major university or holding off on that brand new car. Debt and wealth do not go together, so the sooner you rid yourself of debt, the sooner you can build your own wealth. As mentioned earlier, planning can not only allow you to get out of debt, but it can also help you avoid it altogether. Get into the habit of planning for larger purchases before they occur.

Don't wait until your child goes to college to begin saving for it. Don't wait to graduate to come up with a debt plan. Because of planning, outside of student loans, I have never incurred any debt, despite having owned several cars and buying a home at the age of 19. And never once, during that time, did I make more than minimum wage. Only patience and planning will get you to the next level. I was able to do these things because I wasn't drowning in credit card debt, and I had a savings plan prior to making huge purchases.

Debt doesn't have to be a death sentence; you can climb out if you have a defined plan. The best choice, however, is to lessen your debt load by as much as you can and preparing prior to major expenses.

CHAPTER FOUR

The Wealth Blueprint

I'm an avid reader. During summers, when I was in college, I would read two to three books a week, often finishing one book per day when I wasn't interning. If I don't have my highlighter, sticky notes, and pen with me, I refuse to read. When reading books on personal finance however, I often run into one of two main problems: either the book is filled with fluff or smothered with statistics and data.

I have a bachelor's degree in Economics, so I'm quite comfortable with all the numbers and graphs, but it's that same content that scares away those who need it most.

I contend that personal finance doesn't have to be rocket science; basic math is all that's required. For that reason, I've purposely kept this book simple yet relevant when it comes to using data.

When it comes to most personal finance books, if it not too top-heavy in information, it's too fluffy with corny lines and affirmations that don't always amount to much.

Yes, I believe that, to become a millionaire, you must start with your mindset and how you think about your money, but even after reciting your daily mantra and writing down your goals for six months, you likely haven't added a dollar to your savings. It's rare to find a book that not only provides valuable information but also tells you exactly how to become wealthy.

Well, ladies and gentlemen, it's now your lucky day. Up until now, I've laid before you why many money problems exist, what happens if you don't solve them, and what wealthy people actually do and believe. Now, I am going to show you exactly how to build wealth, step by step. This portion of the book is intended to help you build a very strong foundation for creating your personal fortune.

Before we begin, there is something that you must know. Your goals and your wealth are for you alone. What is wealthy for one person or family may not be the same level of wealth for you. As an example: for a manager at a McDonald's who gets paid $45,000 per year, "wealthy" may mean $540,000. But for a business owner who makes $90,000 per year, wealthy could be $1.8 million.

This is *personal* finance, and your goals are based on you, your family situation, and your job. Never compare your goals to someone else's. It's not a competition or a race; it's a journey that only you can take.

As we enter this journey, I'd like you to complete one exercise to get in the right frame of mind. Take five minutes, and list below the top five things that are important in your life. Yours may be family, food, shopping, faith, and school, or they might be relationships, travel or fitness. Whatever you feel are the things most important to you list them below.

The 5 most important things in my life:

1 _____

2 _____

3 _____

4 _____

5 _____

Now that you've listed the things that are most important to you, list the top five things you spend the most money on. Feel free to check your online bank account and receipts. List them here:

1 _____

2 _____

3 _____

4 _____

5 _____

James W. Frick, former Vice President for Public Relations at the University of Notre Dame, once said, "Don't tell me what your priorities are. Show me where you spend your money, and I will tell you what they are."

If your top expenses and your values didn't match up, there is a problem. If family and financial independence were important to you, don't you think that your funds should be spent in those areas? What you spend money on is usually what's truly important to you. If your top expenses were credit card payments, dinner with friends, alcohol, the casino, and the movies, then your priorities might be mixed up.

You may be spending too much time trying to impress others and not enough time trying to become financially independent. There is nothing wrong with entertainment (except gambling, because it's a waste of money), but it probably shouldn't be one of your top expenses until you have a strong financial foundation. Where you spend your money is likely where you spend your time.

Retail therapy only benefits those who are taking your money. If losing your money is a form of relaxation, it's no wonder you're broke. The time you spend planning and budgeting is directly related to how financially successful you will become.

There are 8,760 hours in a year. Those who build true wealth spend 1 out of every 87 hours planning and budgeting, while those who have high incomes but little to no wealth spend 1 out of every 160 hours planning and budgeting. You don't have to stay glued to your bank account, but it wouldn't hurt to check your balance and budget an hour or two every week. Those who are in love with shopping are usually afraid to check their accounts and absolutely cringe at the thought of budgeting. Keep these people out of your circle and far from your wallet. You don't need *expensive* friends.

Now that we have that out of the way, let's unveil your ultimate plan for building your fortune.

The Wealth Plan

The most effective plans always identify a starting point and an end point and specifically outline the distance and strategies for getting from point to point in between. We know the goal is wealth, but what is it, what does it mean, and exactly how much money is "wealthy" for you?

The technical definition of wealth is "an abundance of valuable possessions or money." This definition itself doesn't do us much good. After all, what is "an abundance," and what is considered "valuable?" Each of those terms is up to one's interpretation. Personally, I like Chris Rock's definition (paraphrasing):

"You can't get rid of wealth. Wealth is passed on, and wealth makes other people rich. Rich you can spend in a day. Shaq is rich, Kobe is rich, but the man that signs their check ... that's wealthy!"

Rock makes a few good points: first, that wealth should be passed on and shouldn't disappear overnight or a few years. That's why you've seen me emphasize the term "true wealth." Many lottery winners and entertainers do not achieve this; they're simply rich – and rich won't last. Rock also makes a point that wealth makes other people rich. This is true. The wealth that you achieve could one day fund your children's or grandchildren's educations; it could help them buy houses or help you start a business that your family takes over. Only real wealth has the ability to do that, because wealth is long-term.

That brings me to Wealth Principle #1:
Don't think about the next day, think about the next decade.

To build wealth, you will need to look ahead. The farther ahead you plan, the wealthier you become. Those who suffer from bad spending habits and credit card debt usually have a short-term outlook. There have been many studies that have recorded the effects of short- and long-term thinking when it comes to how you manage your money, and long-term, patient thinking always wins.

An Experiment

Psychologist Walter Mischel gave preschoolers a tough choice: eat one marshmallow now, or wait for two marshmallows. He found that those who were best able to delay their gratification had higher social skills, self-confidence, and SAT scores as teenagers.[17]

What do marshmallows have to do with your money? Well, to build wealth, you need to create the habit to save money, which requires quite a bit of self-control (even more so when there is a much shinier new Apple product to play with). To delay gratification is to have self-control. It's being able to slow down or delay the things you may really want until you are financially stable enough to obtain them.

It's why people overspend; they want their toys, food, and clothes so badly now that they don't realize or notice how it's going to affect them down the line. The inability to delay will lead to impatience and certain financial death.

What does delayed gratification look like? When I first moved to Dallas to teach, several new teachers, along with myself, scrambled to find housing in the area, armed mostly with any leftover college graduation money, cash from mom or dad, or transitional funding provided by our program.

---

[17] Zweig, J. (2007). Your money and your brain: how the new science of neuroeconomics can help make you rich. New York: Simon & Schuster.

The funding had to be repaid, and we were not going to receive our first paycheck for another 6 to 8 weeks. I needed to either find an apartment and furniture immediately or be homeless in a relatively unfamiliar city.

This was the situation for about 190 Teach for America Corps Members in the summer of 2012. This was also the time that some of us made crucial mistakes. Instead of waiting until the first paycheck or buying furniture sets in pieces, some bought their entire decor in one instant: couch, table, bed, chairs, pots, and pans. Everything was furnished within one or two days of moving, including a flat screen and DVR. How did a fresh college grad afford all of this before receiving his or her first paycheck? It's a two-word answer: credit card.

Some financed their entire apartment on one or two credit cards instead of buying just the essentials. Meanwhile, I used my savings to cover my first month's rent, slept on an air mattress given to me by mother, and bought a used table and chair set in cash. With patience and savings, I was able to furnish the entire house by December. That's delayed gratification. It's having the self-control and discipline to wait and prepare for things rather than to buy on impulse. You will see that much of your ability to build wealth correlates to your ability to control your urges. That skill will make the all-important task of budgeting much easier.

Now that we know what skills it will take to build wealth, let's start to put some numbers to it: wealth, after all, is tied to a specific number; this number, though, is and will always be tied to you and your income. Building wealth is not a race and does not compare itself to others and their progress. Because that is the case, there is no magic number. Two million dollars is not wealthy to some, especially if their expenses well exceed that. For a waiter, however, that amount may be more than enough to be considered wealthy.

There are two metrics or rules that we will use to determine and define wealth. Charles Farrell, author of *Your Money Ratios*, suggests that, in order to retire, you need to have accumulated 12 times your income.

This is our base number for wealth. Take your annual salary, multiply it by 12, and you should have your minimum wealth number *before age 65*.

Someone making $45,000 would need to have at least $540,000. (45,000 x 12).

Most wouldn't look at $540,000 and call it small, but it is a long way from $1 million. It is for this reason that the 12 times your salary figure is the bare minimum. When talking about wealth, you will need at least 12 times your income to even be in the conversation.

With this number, you should be able to retire with minimal worries, no matter what your profession. If you can save 12 times your income, you are certainly a financially successful person.

Wealth, though, has an age quality to it. As a high school student growing up in Oklahoma, a part-time job paying $10 an hour was a pretty good gig. But having that kind of pay ten years later, at 28 years old, wouldn't be so hot anymore.

True wealth should grow as you do; it should never stand still and certainly never recede. Below is a chart (requiring no complex math) that will give you a better idea of what wealth is in terms of numbers.

Wealth Grid

Your Age	Well-off	Rich	Wealthy
Instructions	Multiply your age by 5000	Multiply "well off" by 3	Multiply "Rich" by 3
Age 30	150,000	450,000	1,350,000
Age 50	250,000	750,000	2,250,000

You should always use the 12 times your salary method first. The wealth grid is a rule of thumb; it's a great guide, but not an end-all, be-all. Your wealth will ultimately be affected by how much you bring in and how much you save from that. After you have calculated that number and you feel safe in achieving it, then aim for the next highest bracket.

Notice again how, as your age changes, so should your wealth. A 17-year-old kid would only need $255,000 to be wealthy, but by age 50, that same person would only be well-off. Find what your base wealth number should be, and then find out where you are in terms of your age. This should give you a very good picture of where you want your finances to end up.

Combining both measures of wealth, a 55 year old person making $80,000 per year would need $960,000 to safely retire, $275,000 to be well-off, $825,000 to be rich, and $2,475,000 to be wealthy.

Aiming for the 12 times your salary rule will always put you in prime position to achieve your financial goals; which is why it should be used as the primary figure.

The wealth grid puts your financial goals into perspective and gives you a number to shoot for once you have enough money to retire.

So, what can I do with wealth? What's the point?

I think this is a question that we don't ask ourselves enough. What is the reason for striving to be wealthy? What does wealth do for us, and what should we do with it? Just because you may achieve your base wealth number, you don't get a trophy for it, and you won't be a trending topic on Twitter.

Most people would think that the point of being wealthy is to buy any- and everything you want, to take vacations all around the world, first-class. While you may be able to do this, it's not the *goal* of wealth. Nor is just having money for the sake of it the goal, either.

The fact that we don't know the purpose of wealth is one of the main causes of why there are so few wealthy among us today. Not only are we distracted by the money lies, but we also don't see a real need to build true wealth, because we don't know its purpose. The goal of being wealthy is *mobility* – particularly the ability to move from working every day for money to making your money work for you.

Most people, in America and the world, earn their money in one way: they work for it. It's a simple strategy. Get a job, work hard, and get paid. That's being a laborer. You are being paid for the value of your work. The better you do, the better you get paid. Yet, it can only work for so long. From CEOs to seed farmers, you won't be able to work forever, nor should you have to.

Very few people in the U.S. are able to move from this laborer category to the investor corner. Investors are paid from the *use of their money.* You are simply making your money work for you. No nine-to-five or dealing with a boss –our money makes you more money. That's the goal of being wealthy. While your money is doing all of the work, you're able to spend time with your family, get into new hobbies, and yes, travel, all while your bank account is growing. Being an investor or making your money work for you is sometimes known as passive income; it's the money you make without being there to make sure it happens.

What does this investor/passive income look like? It could come from stocks and bonds. It could also come from interest payments from the bank or money from rental properties that you own. For example, at a car auction, you buy a car for $2500. You park it in your driveway, and after a few weeks, someone makes you an offer for the car. You then sell it for $3500. They decide to pay you $150 per month until it's paid off. That monthly paycheck is passive income: that's how you become an investor. The original $2500 has made you an extra $1000 without you asking your boss for a bonus. Investors do this at a large scale.

At 14, my brother and I became investors with the help of our father. We pulled together our savings from the red Folger's can and bought an Isuzu Amigo from an auction. We sold it to our cousin, who paid us bi-weekly. This process continued until I bought my own car in cash and eventually bid on a foreclosed home five years later.

Building Wealth

Step 1: Setting a goal

With any achievable goal, you need to have a clear starting point and ending point. Your starting point is your current salary and savings, and your ending point can be found in the wealth calculation section. By using these, you have already accomplished a very realistic, simple, measurable, and timely goal.

To be effective in building wealth, the first and perhaps most important thing to do is to get your priorities straight. Having your priorities in order will give you some perspective on the things you are likely to spend money on and help you build your budget and future plans.

Remember that your goal is to build wealth. You are trying to be financially independent, not trying to impress others. "Independence over impression" should be your mantra.

Additionally, you can use the SEE exercise found on page 45. You should focus and budget your attention and cash on the things you felt were important to you in the exercise. Because shoes, luxury cars, and Louis Vuitton are not the most important things in your life, they shouldn't dominate your money or your attention.

Also, setting strong priorities can help you fend off retail temptations. The difference between those who start savings accounts and those waiting in line for shoes are their priorities; two hundred dollars can go a long way – it's just how you use it that matters. Once you have your priorities lined up, you can move to step two: budgeting.

Step 2: Budgeting

You may be able to achieve a high income without budgeting, but you certainly won't be able to create or maintain wealth. If getting a high income is offense, then a great budget is defense. Remember that wealth is what you have left, not what you bring in or what you spend. The only way to ensure you have anything left is to budget. Too often, people are too caught up in playing offense that they forget about their defensive budgeting skills. This is not a smart way to live financially. In this case, the great sports mantra, "Defense wins championships," holds true – and your championship ring will be your wealth.

According to Dr. Stanley, "The foundation stone of wealth accumulation is defense, and this defense should be anchored by budgeting and planning." He continues by stating that today's millionaires became so by budgeting and controlling their expenses, and they maintained their affluent status the same way. You will always need to budget – *always*. You will never reach a point where you are so rich that you won't need to budget for your expenses. You are also never too broke to budget, either.

It will be much easier to create and stick to a budget if you visualize the long-term benefits and effects. It is for that reason that setting your priorities is the first things you need to do in your personal wealth plan.

Creating the budget

Now that you know that budgeting is imperative, how you do create one? Budgeting, at the simplest level, is keeping track of how much money is going in and how much is coming out. Fortunately for you, this is the digital era. In the past, budgeting was much more of a hassle and had to be done by hand, with a calculator and paper. There was no way around it. Today, it can be done in less than ten minutes. Your goal in budgeting should be to make sure that you have money left over from each paycheck. When you don't budget, you cannot be sure exactly how much you spent or how much you have left to spend.

For those new to budgeting, the following will serve as a bare-bones guide to creating a solid budget. For those with more experience, make sure to skim this section to strengthen any budgeting weaknesses you may have.

Budgeting toolbox

1) Budget with a calendar handy

One of the best and often overlooked things you will need to build a good budget is a calendar; never budget without one. Forgotten holidays, birthdays, and events that may have a big impact on your finances will absolutely kill your budget.

But budgeting isn't about cutting out all of the fun in your life. Too many people see budgeting as "listing all the things you can't do." Not only is that the wrong way to think about it, it's also not true. Want to go to Miami for spring break? Winter ski trip with the family? Go for it! With a calendar, you can begin saving months in advance and be sure to not only afford the trip, but afford to splurge a bit while on the trip. It's neither good nor healthy to stress about going broke while on vacation.

2) Trim the fat; don't amputate it

When most people hear the word "budget," they think that they need to immediately cut all of the bad and wasteful things they do in an instant, only to find themselves back at their old habits – and often times even worse than they were when they started. Crash budgets are a lot like crash diets: they simply don't work, and in the long run, they tend to do more harm than good. If you are an addictive shopper, I suggest trimming down your habit instead of going cold turkey. For example, if you spend $500 every month on shoes, the first month, I would try to cut it down to $400, then $320, next down to $250, and so on. From there, it should be much easier to control your spending and it is also more feasible than asking a addict to stop altogether overnight. The key is to not cut too much at one time. If you do, you may stress yourself out and binge-spend. Keep your cuts around 20% each time until you reach your desired amount.

3) Use cash

To make sure you are staying within your means you should make it a point to carry cash. When using cash you tend to spend less because, psychologically, your budgeting skills are better. You can see the amount you spend literally leaving your hands. Also, depending on the setting, you are less likely to spend crisp dollar bills because of a sense of pride according to two marketing professors at the University of Winnipeg[18].

According to a study done by Dunn & Bradstreet, people who use credit and debit cards spend between 12-18% more than those who use cash. Also, fast food chain McDonald's found that "transactions rose from $4.50 to $7 when using plastic."[19]

I am not advocating that you should use cash 100% of the time. Due to security concerns, that would not be the best choice, but for small purchases, everyday items, and variable expenses, cash should be used (I'll explain "variable expenses" later.) Carrying the right amount of cash can deter you from spending too much for some items. The other key advantage of using cash is that you do not incur any overdraft fees or interest charges.

3.5) Give yourself a weekly cash allowance

This can be very effective if you commit to using cash. Choose one day a week to head to the ATM, withdraw a few dollars, depending on the size of your pay, and use that to spend

---

[18]   Coy, P. (2012, November 13). Why We Like Crisp, New Dollar Bills. *Bloomberg Business Week.*

[19]   Beattie, A. (2012, March 28). Should You Pay In Cash? *Investopedia.*

during the week. If you run out of money, wait until the next week to purchase anything.

If you have money left over, great! It carries over. Doing this allows you to pace your spending and spend less at the same time. I also suggest choosing the same day at around the same time to create a strong habit.

4) Save first ... always

Yes, we've all heard it before: pay yourself first. It's common knowledge, yet many still ignore it. This is actually becoming a staple in today's society: get good advice, ignore it, and complain later. How many times have we been told that the best way to get into shape, lose weight, and maintain it is to diet and exercise? Probably too many to count, but every year, there is a new diet pill or crash diet that promises quick results without the work. It never fails. What else never fails? The fact that those who did lose weight through most of those programs nearly gain all of it back. MSNBC reports that 80% of people who lose weight from fad dieting will gain it all back within two years. My advice for you is to stick to what you know works, no matter how boring it is.

Most people choose to ignore the classic pay yourself first rule, not because they don't know it exists but because they usually don't have any money left.

"I usually don't have any money left over to save."

You didn't have any money *left over*, but you had money for new shoes, *Fifty Shades of Grey*, Chinese food, and drinks for the game. Sounds like a lie to me.

The word *first* in "pay yourself first" is there for a reason. Just as Uncle Sam makes sure he gets a cut of your check, without fail, every time, you need to do the same. When you say you have no money left to save, it usually means A) you are spending too much on things you may not really need, B) you're living way above your means, or C) you don't have your priorities straight and are attempting to spend 100% of your pay each and every time. There should *never* be an excuse for you not paying you. You pay everyone else, from the government to the gas station, and you should have something in the bank to show for it.

5) Know the difference in spending

One of the biggest skills in budgeting is finding out your expenses. Once you figure this part out, everything about budgeting gets much easier. There are only two parts to your spending: variable expenses and fixed expenses.

Fixed expenses are things that you have to pay every month and whose prices will not change, like rent, medicine, gym memberships, or tithes/donations. You can accurately estimate how much this will cost each month. Though savings is not an expense, per se, I include it in this section, because I know how much I'm going to save from each paycheck, and I want to make sure that I am getting paid, since I am paying everyone else. Also, I feel that it's good to see savings like rent, as something that is mandatory and that must happen, without fail.

Technically speaking you can add another category of spending within fixed expenses called planned expenses. These types of expenses are spaced out over time to avoid creating debt or spending too much money at one time. Starting a Christmas fund for shopping or saving for a summer vacation would be a planned expense.

Variable spending, the second type are things that aren't as predictable. You know you have an electric bill, but the cost may vary – the same with filling up your car. It can be more difficult to estimate these expenses. The key in budgeting is to overestimate. If you normally spend about $100 in gas every month, budget $120-135, just in case. Gas prices could rise, or you may have to run around and drive more than normal one weekend, and you don't want those small things to throw your entire budget off.

6) Add some play money

Budgeting doesn't have to be painful and boring; there is no crime in leaving some money to play with at the end (key word: at the *end*). After you save and after your fixed and variable expenses are taken care of, if you are living within your means, a few dollars should be left over to play with. I call this "play money." It's okay to budget this in. If you budget too tightly, you may become stressed, and this is where many people give up. It can be daunting to count every single penny, so many who do instantly binge once they go a dollar over, because they feel that their entire budgets are worthless.

The reason you want to have play money is twofold: to build a cushion and to reward your efforts. This will help you not to overspend; it's also much less stressful to give yourself an amount to play with. You know that all necessities are taken care of and that you have contributed to your bank account: congrats, you've earned yourself some play money.

Those who don't budget have an entire income of play money, and the Spending Lie begins to take over. Bills may or may not get paid, savings certainly doesn't happen, and credit cards grow faster than weeds in the spring. As a rule of thumb, I suggest that your play money not be larger than 30% of your monthly income. This is a precaution to ensure that you have plenty of money left over in case something comes up: you always want to be on guard for unexpected financial events, good and bad.

Putting it all together

The six tips listed above are not to be taken individually; they are much more powerful when used together. In this section, I will model how you can improve your budget and how to use all six steps to create financial harmony.

If you are starting from scratch with a budget, meaning you've never done it before or you want to start fresh, you have a few options when it comes to using technology to make this process much easier. You can do it by hand (sometimes even in your head) and on paper, but if you make a mistake, it's much harder to correct. You could lose your budgeting sheet, and in short, things can get sloppy. My suggestion to make budgeting easier is to use either Mint or Personal Capital's free budgeting software and apps. The advantage of these sites is that they can text or email you when and if you have overspent.

As you sit down to begin, grab a calendar, and figure out all of your expenses, fixed and variable (as well as any planned expenses). Check to see when your paydays are and what days your bills are due. Begin listing them and their amount either on paper or one of the budgeting programs listed. (Feel free to list on paper first then transfer the information digitally.) Next, find out how much you get paid on a monthly basis.

At this point, you should notice something very important. Is what you're spending bigger than what you're getting paid? If so, you have some things in the expense categories that need to change. If this is your issue, begin to trim some of your variable expenses. Remember, unless you plan to move or you feel that something is no longer necessary, it's a lot harder to cut fixed expenses. Anytime trimming needs to occur, always start with the variable expenses, and remember: trim the fat; don't amputate everything at once.

If you've gotten both numbers to be equal, then you're living right at your means. I would suggest that, long-term, you cut some of your expenses down.

If you are making more money than you are spending, perfect! You're in the right spot. What you have left over is considered your play money. To insure that you don't blow it too quickly, take a small amount of that sum out of the ATM weekly – that is your cash allowance until the next payday.

That's it! Your next job is to be consistent. Rarely does a budget work 100% on the very first try. It takes practice, but budgeting is a skill that, if used well, will never fail you when you begin building your own fortune. Budgeting is a national pastime of the wealthy; practice it, excel at it, and you will have a much smoother road to wealth.

The Quick Budget

One you have mastered the basics of budgeting, you can begin to do it a lot more quickly and with more efficiency. One way to do that is with the 50/20/30 rule: it suggests that 50 percent of your money should be set aside for essentials: mortgage, rent, transportation, groceries, and utilities. Twenty percent goes to financial goals and can be split between your savings and investing accounts, and the remaining 30 percent is yours to spend freely.

Going by this rule will enable you to make better financial decisions, as well. When searching for apartments, if rent alone approaches 50 percent of your pay you know that it is going to be too big of a strain on your budget because of your other necessities. Instead of blindly finding a place to live and figuring out how to afford it afterward; this rule allows you to avoid bad financial commitments before they occur.

This is, again, a rule of thumb; your budget does not have to look exactly like this, but your percentages should be close. You will find that, as you get into the habit of budgeting, the more closely your expenses mirror this rule, the less stressed you will be about your budget! Your money will begin to take care of itself.

Step 3: Build Your Emergency Fund

Once you have your priorities and budget set, your very next monetary goal should be to build your emergency fund. This is an absolute requirement to preserving your wealth and sanity. Accidents happen without warning; they don't care what time you have to be at work, how much you spend on your home, or how much was in it as it burned to the ground. Big or small, accidents *can* kill your mood and murder your money…but it doesn't always have to be that way. Every person should have a fully funded emergency fund, and this should be among your top priorities.

Never let anyone try to talk you into investments or making huge purchases without having an emergency fund first. An emergency fund can help you with transitions between jobs or locations; it can allow you to be closer to family members when needed with a last-minute flight. Getting caught by life without an emergency fund can be expensive and often leads to debt.

So just how big should your emergency fund be? It should be a bare minimum of 10% of your salary. From there you should reach to 3 months' worth your expenses, then grow it to 6 months. There is no specific dollar amount that you should aim for, because it's based on how much you spend.

If you were to lose your job but had a fully funded e-fund, you wouldn't have to resort to panic mode immediately. Why not? Because you could live the exact lifestyle you are living now for 6 months. At month 6, you might start to panic, but by then, you should have found a solution.

You will have to exercise discipline to leave the amount untouched. One way to do that is to put an amount in an online bank. With that, it usually won't be as present in your mind like larger banks that have physical locations.

When your emergency fund reaches 15 percent of your annual salary you should begin to focus your attention to reaching your wealth goal.

Step 4: How Much Should I Save to Reach My Wealth Goal?

For years, the minimum amount that we were taught to save from each paycheck was 10 percent. That is no longer the case. According to Charles Farrell, to reach your base wealth goal of 12 times your income, you need to, at bare minimum, begin saving 12% starting at the age of 25. If you are under the age of 25, go ahead and save 12%, too; you'll be much farther ahead.

From age 45 until retirement (age 65), you should bump up that savings percentage to 15. This is called a savings ratio; below is a chart.

Savings Ratio

Age	Savings Rate
25	12%
30	12%
35	12%
40	12%
45	15%
50	15%
55	15%
60	15%
65	15%

Find your age and your annual salary. When you follow the chart below, it will tell you exactly what to save per month to reach that goal. If you're worried about math, don't fret. The calculations are simple, one you calculate the amount that you need to save per month automate this into a retirement account so that you can save without fail.

Age	Yearly Salary	Amount saved per year	Amount saved per month
Your age	Your annual salary before taxes	Your salary x 12% or 15%	Divide last column by 12
25	$45,000	$5,400	$450
45	$50,000	$7,500	$625

(See, I told you that the math wasn't that bad!)

The more you save today, the more you get to spend later. Remember that these numbers are based on your base wealth goal – if you want to be richer in retirement, feel free to bump up these numbers a bit. Just be sure not to go under them. You may be wondering how $450 a month is going to become $540,000 based on the base wealth goal. It would literally take 100 years to build up to that goal by saving $450 a month! Instead, you should be putting this money into a retirement account such as a 401(k) or Individual Retirement Account. This will allow you to invest your money using compound interest and take advantage of any additional contributions your employer may provide which will make the money you save grow much faster.

For example, if you were to earn $100,000 a year and saved 12 percent of your pay. After the first year you added $12,000 to your retirement account. If you get a 10 percent return on the money you put into the account, $1200 will be added to your original amount making it $13,200. This process continues to accelerate your savings adding up to more than $768,000 in 20 years even though you only put in $240,000. How did you go from putting in $240,000 to ending up with $768,000? Compounding interest: the more you save, the more your money pays you. Even if you were to make $35,000 per year you can reach your base wealth goal if you're saving at least 12 percent and your investments grow at least 7 percent each year. (We'll talk about how to get at least a 7 percent return in the next chapter).

The beauty in using ratios like the ones above is that they automatically change with the change in your income. If you go from making $45,000 a year to $30,000, the amount you would save monetarily would change, but your savings rate would still be at 12 percent. This ensures that you are still saving what you need to reach your base wealth goal. As long as you go by the percentages, you will be fine, no matter what the amount of your salary is. Whether you're working at Wal-Mart or working on Wall Street, the number the proportion of money saved will be the same.

There are two more very important aspects of the numbers above. The first is the amount saved per month. Once you have calculated this number, you will know exactly what you need to save by the time you're ready to retire. But can you really depend on yourself to save that amount every month, no matter what? Is it a guarantee that you won't forget or put a few less dollars in from time to time?

Even the most disciplined savers may falter from time to time, which brings me to my next point. Once you have arrived at the amount you should be saving per month, make these payments automatic. This is called automation, meaning that the amount is automatically taken from your account, almost like your taxes.

This ensures that you cannot fail, forget, or falter. Uncle Sam never forgets to take his cut of your check; with automated payments to your retirement account, you'll never forget to get a piece of your own.

Doing this will guarantee that you reach your goal. Building wealth cannot depend on luck; that is a plan for failure. It is important to employ every resource necessary to build a strong foundation. If you feel that $450 per month is too much to save at one time, you can split that amount into bi-weekly payments to yourself. For some, this is much easier to manage. If this is the case, you would want to automate these payments, as well.

Step 5: Properly managing your debt

The final step to building reliable wealth is to properly manage your debt, good and bad. Recall that there are debts that can be considered good, such as mortgages and loans for education.

Though not all loans of that magnitude are perfect, they carry a reasonably high chance of paying you back more than what you originally borrowed. For example, if you attended a school on a college loan for $50,000, and your salary ends up being $75,000; you took on a good debt and turned it into an investment. The same could be said for houses.

Bad debt, however, does not carry the chance that you can gain more than what you paid for it. You're unlikely to make a profit nearly anything you currently swipe your credit card for. You also open up a door to an endless cycle of payments that, if not paid in full every month, could diminish your ability to build wealth. Managing your debt correctly is simple but not always easy.

Debt Principle #1: Never buy a brand new car

New cars are a waste of money and lose value the second you drive them off the lot. If you are craving a new car, then I suggest that you reread the section on the Spending Lie: you're too caught up in trying to impress people, rather than trying to be financially independent.

Riding around in a new car does not show how rich you *are* but how rich you *were*. That $35,000-40,000 that could have been growing in a bank account is sitting in your garage, losing value.

Don't try to skate by and think that leasing a car is a better option, either. Leasing cars is also a bad option that lends itself to bigger financial problems. Leasing a car might be cheaper in the short run, but it's much more expensive, since you'll presumably lease more cars for as long as you need transportation. Leasing creates an endless cycle of burning your own money.

Buy your cars used and, if at all possible, try to buy them all in cash. If you need to wait an extra year to save up the cash to do so, do it; it's worth it. When I was 14, I bought my first car in cash. It took my 14 years' worth of saving allowance plus my 12-year-old brother's savings to buy it.

We then sold the car and made a profit. This continued until I was 16 and bought my first used car for myself in cash (the one bought at 14 was an investment). To this date, I have never made a car payment in my lifetime, and I've had a total of five vehicles. I don't believe in auto debt; it's unnecessary.

In fact, those who are so caught up in trying to show off their cash are likely displaying a need for recognition and power rather than the money itself. As I was walking out of Wal-Mart, a black car approached me with the tinted window rolled down to reveal two women in the front seat. "Hey, would you happen to have like $4? We really need gas money," one said with a smile. I patted my pockets, as if I had nothing, knowing I had 21 dollars in my left pocket at the time.

Instead, I went to my car and offered $2.25. Both smiled and drove away. As I continued to put groceries in my car, a 2000 Mazda 626, I couldn't help but wonder, "How can they afford to drive a 2013 Cadillac CTS with customized all black rims but can't afford a gallon of gas?" The perceived need to drive nice cars and wear nice clothes without the proper finances is a common practice that will keep you dependent on a paycheck.

As long as you're trying to impress, you will always be broke.

Debt Principle #2: Use your credit card sparingly.

You must be very, very careful about how you use your credit card, not only for financial reasons but professional reasons, as well. Some companies check your credit history before considering you for a position. In 2010, according to CNN, 60% of employers run credit checks on some or all of their candidates, which is up from 43% in 2006 and 25% in 1998; the trend is likely to continue. Not only will mismanaging your finances keep you broke, but it could also have you jobless, as well.

Why do employers care so much about how you manage your money? Some of it may be due to the nature of the position. If you're going into any job dealing with money – financial broker, adviser, accountant, etc. – how can you be trusted to look over someone else's finances if you can't do well on your own? Having someone with bad credit manage money would be like an obese doctor advising you to lose weight. You've got to practice what you preach. Another reason employers may check is that, if you are in serious debt, you may be under constant fire from bill collectors, which could distract you on the job.

To keep your credit under control, there are three simple rules you need to follow:

1 Pay your balance in full every month. When you do not, you incur interest charges from the credit card company. What you originally bought for $200 could end up costing $250 or more because you didn't pay it off in full. If you are thinking of swiping for something, ask yourself if you can pay it all when the bill is due. If you cannot, you have no business buying it.

2 Use your card for fixed expenses. You are going to be in debt if you are using your card for buying gas, food, and other expenses that are hard to predict. This is precisely why many credit card companies offer rewards on these items. They know that you spend more when you use plastic, and they know that, as long as you can't see the totals adding up, you won't be able to pay in full. What a smart move by them – but you're smarter. Use your card to buy things like monthly prescriptions, cable bills, or membership fees. These bills are likely to be low, and the cost won't change. For the other items, strictly use cash.

3 Never go over 20% of your credit card limit (10% is ideal). How much of your available credit you use can seriously affect your score. It could also be an indicator of how much you are overspending. If your credit limit is $1000, never charge more than $200 to it. The more of your credit you use, the more desperate you look on paper. The more of your limit that you use beyond 20%, the lower your credit score becomes.

Debt Principle #3: Be smart about college loans.

With the skyrocketing cost of higher education and rising standards from employers, it's almost impossible to begin a stable career without the help of a college degree. In fact, due to the growing popularity and seemingly ubiquitous sentiment that college is expected, it has been predicted that the bachelor's degree will soon become the equivalent of a high school diploma.

Those without an athletic gift who may have missed out on other scholarships will have to take on debt to obtain a higher education. This isn't necessarily bad, but it can be, if you're not smart about it.

In the summer of 2010, I was fortunate to earn a spot in an internship program allowing college students to work in New York City's highest financial firms.

A portion of the program was a series of bi-weekly meetings with different CEOs of large firms such as Drefuys and MetLife. We would all gather around with notepads in large board rooms, jotting down the wisdom of each executive we met as if it were scripture.

In each meeting, there was time for questions, and inevitably, the same question would be asked from one of the interns: "Is it more important to get an MBA now, right after undergrad, or is it best to work for a few years first?" Of the 20 or so interns, about 16 total were a part of an extended undergraduate program that allowed them to earn an MBA at the end of their fifth year.

Every CEO said more or less the same thing; one of the most memorable quotes was this: "I could care less about where you graduated from. I want to know if you can do the work. That's what it comes down to. Harvard, Yale, it doesn't matter. I will take someone with great work experience over a Harvard MBA any day of the week. Work experience and school experience are two different things."

Every week, one of the MBA students would ask that same question, and every week, a different CEO would echo the same response. It's not always about the name of the school but how you can sell yourself, your experiences, and your employment history. Proven results are always better than theory. What makes a good student doesn't always make a great employee or leader ... or millionaire. According to Dr. Stanley's research, with the exception of attorneys and physicians (19% of the total millionaire population),

America's most wealthy had an undergraduate GPA between 2.76 and 2.92.

When it comes to taking out college loans, be smart. The school you come from isn't the most important thing and may not be worth the debt. If the same program is offered cheaper at a community college or state school, you may want to seriously consider it. Remember, your education is for you; it's not to impress others with where you went to school. And just because a university has a big name doesn't mean that it's better. Consider this excerpt from Charles Wheelan's book, *Naked Economics*:

> … Mr. Kruger and Ms. Dale took their research analysis one step further. They examined the outcomes of students who were admitted to both a highly selective schools and moderately selective schools. Some students headed to places like the Ivy League; others chose their less likely option … The average earnings of students admitted to both a highly selective school and a moderately selective school were roughly the same, regardless of which type of college they attended. Mr. Kruger offers this advice to students applying to college: "Don't believe that the only school worth attending is the one that will not admit you … Recognize that your own motivation, ambition and talents will determine your success more than the college name on your diploma."

Think twice about taking out massive loans for college. The education and experience is certainly worth it, but the debt, may not be. Even though education can be considered a good debt depending on your field of study, it does not grant you a license to take on as many loans as possible. Try to avoid college debt as much as you can.

Conclusion

You now have a solid plan for building wealth and managing your money. Following the instructions laid out in this chapter will ensure that you keep your debt to a minimum, save enough money for retirement, and budget responsibly and stress-free. As long as you keep your priories in order and automate your savings, you should have no problem creating a strong financial foundation.

Saving and budgeting alone, no matter how consistent, will get you to your wealth goal. You will need to make your money grow. Up until now, I haven't been specific as to how to actually grow your money. It's because without this foundation, without an emergency fund and budgeting, skipping straight to investing can be extremely dangerous. In the next chapter, I will decode the world of Wall Street and unveil some ways to invest outside of the stock market, too.

CHAPTER FIVE

Investing Made Simple

Managing your finances is a journey. It's like planting a seed: you take care of it, water it, and, over time, a tree will grow, and you can live off of the fruit. It's not a fast process, nor is it a particularly fun one to sit down and watch, but if you take care of it, it will last for generations.

Well, that's how wealth building *should* be, but for many, it is not. Too many people have fallen in love with the quick dollar. Buying and selling stocks within hours or flipping houses within weeks looks great for some people and can appear impressive. Can some of these strategies work? In short, yes, but the level of necessary expertise, stress, and risk isn't worth it for many of the people who pursue it.

One of the biggest barriers to investing is its complexity. There are too many terms to understand and too many numbers to digest, and by the time you learn them, everything has changed. What companies should you buy? When should you sell? These, not to mention the fear of losing money, are among the questions that turn people away from investing in the stock market. If any of these questions have crossed your mind, if you've been cautious or afraid of investing in stock, this chapter is for you.

As a math teacher, I know firsthand how the sound of numbers and calculations can intimidate kids … and parents. Upon reading this chapter, you will walk away with a much better understanding of the market – what it is and how to play it safe while still building your fortune – as well as investing outside the stock market. You can put your security blanket away now. Let's begin.

"I Don't Understand Stocks"

Go back for a moment to when you were 16 years old; you've just passed your driver's test. You are a confident driver, and you know exactly how to get from point A to point B. The steps are simple: start the car, put on your seat belt, hands at ten and two, use your signal, and (for some) obey the speed limit. Pretty simple. But, at that time – and even now – did you know what the cam shaft is? What about the catalytic converter? Do you know how the engine mounts affect the car? Chances are, you didn't know any of that when you were 16 and, unless you are a mechanic, you may not know much about that right now (without the help of Google).

Despite your ignorance, you do still know how to drive the car from point A to point B, right? You know when the car needs gas or if the tire is flat. You don't need to know every single tidbit of the car and its inner workings; you just need to know the basics. That same principle applies when it comes to investing. Unless you are a day trader or Wall Street broker, you probably don't need to know every single little thing under the sun to be a good investor. You only need to get from point A: where you are now, to point B: wealth.

Spend just 10 minutes on MSNBC, or flip through the *Financial Times*. You can get lost very quickly without a finance degree – but the same can be said if you were flipping through a mechanic's manual, too, and that doesn't mean that you can't drive the car.

Those on Wall Street may tell you differently. They'll say that it takes a professional to navigate the market; it's too complex. They will say that the experts are better. Well, statistics say otherwise; in Jason Zweig's book, *Your Money, Your Brain*, he unveils the following truths about the so-called "financial experts":

- Every December, *Business Week* surveys Wall Street's leading strategists. Over the past decade, the consensus of these experts' predictions have been off by an average of 16%.
- Wall Street analysts who carefully study a handful of stocks might as well be playing eeny meeny miny moe. Over the past 30 years, the analysts' estimates of what companies would earn in the next quarter have been wrong by an average of 41%. That's like the weatherman saying it's going to be 60 degrees tomorrow, and it turns out that it's 35 degrees. How much longer would you listen to him?

These "experts" and analysts are wrong often. Everyone thinks they have an edge or a specialization that will make their predictions and estimates better than the next, but it's all the same.

You've probably noticed that those who said Facebook would be the next Google stock turned out to be wrong. Those who said that the housing market would never fail? Wrong again. They are all fads and trends and, just like Pokémon cards and shoes with pop-out wheels, they'll fade with time, often when you least expect it.

So, why are these people still on TV? Why do so many still listen to them? Many do it because of what I mentioned above. They believe that investing is too complicated for them to tackle on their own and that they need someone to guide them.

This is not to say that you won't need help, because everyone does at some point, but investing is not rocket science.

The other reason that many people continue to follow these "experts" is simply because their stats aren't often listed. Think about it. How do you see whether or not a stock pitch man was right? There is a conscious effort to ignore the bad stock picks and boost the few that were correct. No one wants to show off their report card if there are Cs and Ds.

Lastly, many people listen to the experts because it seems like a quick and fast way to make money – and it can be. But it's not always the most reliable. It's just like crash dieting: it may work for a few weeks, but after a while, you will get burned. In this case, it's your cash that can go up in flames. The entertainment factor of Wall Street is alluring for many. Saying the words "Wall Street," delivers a level of prestige, savviness, and sophistication.

You can get so caught up in fancy vocabulary, numbers, and the day-to-day losses and gains that you forget about what actually works and what is happening in the long run. Remember: wealth starts out as a seed. If you plant a seed tonight and wake up in the morning to nothing more than a moist spot in the ground where you watered, are you going to panic? No, of course not. You know that it takes time, but those on Wall Street would be in a frenzy. There, it's usually about quick money and how much was made by four p.m., not how much was made in four years.

What Is "The Market"?

You've probably noticed the flashing numbers and ticker symbols scroll across the bottom of your TV screen, or maybe you've seen the red and green arrows in the top corner of the newspaper. These are indicators of the market. They give us a day-to-day snapshot of how the economy is doing and, if you're an investor, how well your investments are doing. But what exactly do those numbers mean, and how do you make sense of them? These two questions alone turn away thousands of potential investors, thus cutting off one of the best avenues to wealth.

The stock market, at its heart, is simple. Let's pick a company – say, Wal-Mart. If you were the Wal-Mart creator starting from the ground up or wanting to expand, imagine how much money you would need. Considering the cost of the store, all of the inventory, baskets and carts, scanners, employees, etc., you would need millions just to get started.

Would you rather build all of it out of your own pocket, or would you like to use other people's money? The answer is simple: you'd much rather go shopping with someone else's money than your own.

So, how do you raise enough funds from people to build and expand these stores? That's where stocks come in. Wal-Mart sells stock, or a small piece of its company, to raise money for its projects. The benefit is mutual: Wal-Mart gets money to build more stores and you get a small piece of Wal-Mart. If the company is successful and continues to grow, you can sell those pieces for a profit.

That's pretty much it – the basics, at least. (Of course, there are many more intricacies, but again, you don't need to be a mechanic.) The market itself is a collection of companies, large and small, trying to raise money to fuel their businesses. The stock price is the cost of one piece of that company. As of writing, the stock price of Wal-Mart is $69.20, so for that amount, you can become an owner of Wal-Mart (albeit a very, very small owner). If you hold on to that piece and the price goes up, you can sell it and make money.

For example, on September 11, 1998, the price of Wal-Mart stock was around $15. If you had bought one share then and sold it today for $69.20, you would have made $54.20. This is just an example – when you're actually investing, you buy hundreds of shares, not just one, so the profit you would make would be multiplied by the number of shares that you buy.

The stock market refers to a collection of companies and people who are buying and selling stocks. You can imagine it like an elementary school cafeteria, with kids walking around trying to trade their sandwiches for cookies. Some snacks are in high demand, while others are not. The same could be said with stocks: some, such as Apple, are in high demand as the world anxiously awaits what they'll come up with next.

Now that we know what the stock market is, how do we measure it? What tells us if things are good or bad? That's called an index and, in the U.S., the most popular index is called the Dow Jones Industrial Average. The Dow, as it's commonly referred to (also known as "the Market") is a collection of the 30 biggest companies in the U.S. Going back to our school analogy, it could be seen as the "popular kid" average. Simply put, the Dow Jones uses a formula to average the prices of the 30 biggest companies, and that tells us how well the economy is doing as a whole. It tells many investors whether to buy or sell their stocks. The Dow is expressed as a number and changes every minute of every weekday from 9:30 a.m. until 4 p.m Eastern time.

But what about the rest of the companies? How can 30 companies tell millions of investors what to do and think, and since when did the popular kids represent the trends and attitudes of the whole school?! Well, in actuality, it doesn't. The Dow is the oldest and most recognized index, but it doesn't always give us a complete picture. There are several other indexes, two of which are very popular: the S&P 500 and NASDAQ. We'll focus most of our attention on the S&P 500 for now. It was created by a company called Standard and Poor's in 1957. It's basically an average of the 500 largest companies in the U.S. – a much broader measure of how an entire school is doing, rather than just the popular crowd. Like the Dow, its number fluctuates throughout the day.

Why stocks and indexes fluctuate so much throughout the day is a much more complicated issue that we can attribute more to the popularity of some companies, laws that get (or will maybe get) passed, and sometimes even the weather. As you'll see in later sections, and as we've learned in previous chapters, you needn't be too concerned with the day to day operations and fluctuations of the market; focus on the long-term outlook.

Bonds

Another way in which companies can decide to raise money for their operations is in taking out a loan from you, otherwise known as a bond. A bond is a contract from a company that promises to pay you back a certain amount by a certain time. Not only do companies do this, but cites, schools, states, and even the U.S. government participate. Bonds are generally more reliable than stocks because they typically do not move in price each day.

Stocks have the potential to lose value, bonds are fixed (you are 100% guaranteed to be paid back 100% of a U.S. bond) but they are not as potentially profitable as stocks. While you could make or lose $50 for every share of Wal-Mart, you may only make $10 for every bond you buy.

If you can't make as much money from bonds, why do people buy them, and why do companies offer them? Companies may offer them because they don't want to cede ownership, and individuals buy bonds because they are less likely to lose their money.

If you buy a stock that loses money, the company owes you nothing; in buying a bond, the company's promise to pay you back is almost guaranteed. The reason it's not fully guaranteed is that companies can fail or default on their bond. The U.S. government is the only entity in which you are 100% guaranteed to get your money back when you buy a bond.

To become a successful investor, you need to combine a mix of stocks and bonds, because you never want to put all of your eggs in one basket. Now that you have a basic understanding of how stocks and bonds work, how safe is it to put your money in these investments? In which companies should you put your money, and how often should you check on your stocks? These are very important questions that mean the difference between becoming wealthy or going broke.

Is It Safe?

The year is 1971. Two brothers approach you with a unique investing opportunity. They want to give you shares of their company in exchange for some start-up money. You examine their business plan, see that it is profitable, and decide to make the exchange. Over the next 30 years, the company becomes huge. What started as a small company in Ann Arbor, Michigan has now gone international. It's the year 2000, and this company's name is Borders – yes, the second-largest bookselling giant. You may know or be able to predict what happens next: the digital age comes and changes the game for many booksellers. While Borders and many others did not adapt quickly enough, its competitor, Barnes and Noble, did. To date, only Barnes and Noble and Books A Million have survived.

If you were that 1970s investor, you would have been extremely rich during the first 20 years or so. But if you had not gotten out and instead held onto your original stock, your money would have disappeared along with the Borders company. Buying stocks can be risky, because you never know what's around the corner. What may be extremely popular and profitable now may not be so in the future.

No one can predict the future and which companies may or may not fail. Usually, success and failure result from unexpected events that have very costly impacts. Take two very popular companies now, Amazon and Apple. I am a fan of Amazon as a customer, but in the next 20 years, what happens if the Internet is no longer necessary? What if another website comes along with better prices? These are unknowns that affect whether or not an investor will be financially successful. Though Apple is incredibly popular now, what if it's a fad and the world finds something newer and shinier to play with down the line?

When thinking about stocks, safety is a real concern. How you can protect your wealth is a serious question that needs to be addressed. To that, I offer this scenario: which is better, to bet on the success of one football team to win it all or to bet on the entire league? Would you rather bet on the odds of a single card or own the entire deck? I think the answer is obvious. It's much safer and practical if you can own the whole thing. When it comes to sports in particular, you can't lose. No matter which team is playing on the field, the stadium always wins.

The moral is this: why consume yourself with trying to pick the right company and worrying about its longevity day in and day out when you could just own the entire stock market? At first glance, you may wonder, "How in the world can I own every stock?" The answer to that is quite simple. You can own the entire market by investing in an index fund, such as the S&P 500 Index. By buying this fund, you own each of its 500 companies. As the index goes up, so does your wealth. Index funds don't seek to beat the market, they simply match it.

How safe is it? As far as stocks go, it's one of the safest, most productive investments out there. You won't be so caught up in trying to beat the market and trying to get the best gains. You won't have to monitor the news and sell your stock just to buy it back the next week. Once you buy it, you may sit still, relax, and let the index fund do all the work. Sound boring? Yes, but it also sounds wealthy. All the Wall Street jargon about how to beat the market and which stocks are hot will have no effect on you; it becomes white noise. In fact, by investing in an index fund, you are automatically better than the majority of other investors.

John Bogle cites the editor of the Heubert financial digest in his book, *The Little Book of Common Sense Investing*. After monitoring the records of financial advisors for 26 years, they concluded that "you can outperform 80% of your fellow investors over the next several decades by simply investing in an index fund and nothing else." In addition to that, Warren Buffet, the second wealthiest man in the U.S., believes that index funds are the way to go for most individuals.

There will be times when this investment will lose money and could do so for a period of time, but the key is in looking long-term. Let's say you could invest in the weather. For every sunny day, your wealth grows; every rainy day, it declines. There will be days where there is not a cloud in the sky, but it's almost impossible to have zero days of rain. In fact, there could be several rainy days within a week. But over the course of the year, there are almost always more sunny days than rainy days.

That's how you have to look at index funds. Wall Street experts panic at the sight of rain. They live on a day-to-day basis and ask themselves, "How much did I make today? How much did I lose?" A patient index investor is not worried with each day's weather but the climate as a whole. "So what if it rained today? I live in San Diego. It'll be warm and sunny before you know it." That is the thought of an index investor: patient, calm, collected, and always looking toward the next decade – not the next day.

How Much Should I Invest?

The goal of becoming wealthy is not to work for money but instead to make it work for you. This can happen in several different ways, but the main vehicle I am speaking about is stocks and bonds. They are the mainstream, most reliable, low-maintenance ways to grow your money.

We have already discussed what stocks, bonds, and index funds are. Now, it's time to unveil how much of each and what investment option you should use to build wealth. You should never try to use too much of one strategy, because nothing is 100% reliable 100% of the time. I suggest that you do not concern yourself with trying to buy individual stocks.

Too often, the research, rebalancing, and constant changes are too much to keep track of, and the success rates versus a basic index fund are low over the long run. There are and will always be some individual companies that seem to always make money (Google and Apple are two), but just because they have a history of growth does not mean that their futures will show the same.

It's human nature to be confident in the things we invest ourselves in, from our money to our sports teams, and it's that confidence that can sometimes derail your wealth. We are not good predictors of the unknown and unforeseen. We should expect the unexpected and try our best to guard against it. For example, Borders was a very strong and reputable company. From its founding years in the 1970s until the 1990s, no one would have thought that some things called the "Internet" and "e-readers" could have destroyed this company; it had been doing so well for so long. However, this plight could hit any company, and investing all of your money into one is never a good strategy, regardless of the history.

This is why I suggest index funds that track the S&P 500. You are not investing in one sole company but 500 different ones. If one fails, you're not set too far back, and it is highly unlikely that all will lose money at the same time. This is called diversification; it's spreading your money across different investments to balance out the low points that you may have.

An index fund is about as diversified as you can get. The best part about it is that you will not be concerned with day-to-day headlines of the market; nor will you need to do hours and hours of research. This is an investment that you can virtually set and forget.

If this so-called investment is so reliable, why don't many people talk about it? The reason why you don't hear too much about index funds in the news is basically the same reason why you don't hear that one-third of millionaires are teachers, engineers, middle managers, and accountants who drive Ford F-150s: it's boring. They spend less than what they make, don't live in huge houses and believe in long-lasting marriages.

These common sense principles needed in life aren't always what's entertaining. No one wants to hear about reliable diversification and building wealth slowly, because quick cash and trading stocks is much more fun and risky. But do you want to risk a wealthy retirement for pizzazz?

Another reason these types of investments aren't as popular is because those who sell these funds are not compensated as much. Remember I mentioned that this was a "set it and forget it" type of investment. Because of that, investment companies don't need to constantly check up on it or tweak it to make it better; therefore, they are not paid as much as they are to sell other stocks and funds. As a broker, you want to perform your ethical duties, but you also want to keep the lights on. Often times, they'll show you what *might* work for a high price rather than what *will* work for much cheaper.

Though an index fund is the best investment option to grow your wealth, it is not invincible. With the index fund, your money is expected to grow between 9-13 percent on average

– some years are better, some worse. With $1000 invested one time in an S&P 500 index, earning 11 percent would grow to $13,585 in 25 years and $184,565 in 50 years. And that's just one time; imagine what you could do if you followed the Savings Rule and invested 12 percent in this index every year! It's almost too easy to become wealthy this way. However, as stated, the 9-13 percent number is an *average*. U.S. companies are not perfect. Take 2008, after the housing crisis, or 2001, after September 11th. Index funds likely did not reach these numbers in those years. The chances are that it did recover well; however, it is not a guarantee that it will win every single year.

The U.S. stock market works in cycles. There are great times of boom and bad times of busts. It's called the business cycle; no one period will last forever, no matter how good or bad things may seem. Historically, stocks make money two-thirds of the time and lose money one-third of the time. So, in any one year, you have a 67 percent chance that your index fund is going to make you money but a 33 percent chance that it is not. In the years that it doesn't make money, do you sit there and take it? No. That's where bonds come in.

Usually, when stocks aren't doing so hot, bonds do well, and vice versa. Also, since index funds aren't guaranteed to give you a return, it's best to have a backup plan; bonds are solid backups. When you begin to invest, you must split your money between your index fund and bonds. How much you split between the two is up to you. There are a few different schools of thought.

One theory, provided by Charles Farrell, is that you should split the money you have set aside for retirement down the middle, half in stocks and half in bonds, until you reach age

55; then, you should have 40 percent of your money in stocks and the remaining 60 percent in bonds. It is customary to reduce your stock holdings as you get older. Recall that 33 percent of the time, you could lose money – it is much easier to take that risk at age 25 than 65, because you have a much higher chance of making money over the long run when you are young. As you age, you don't want to take on that much risk, nor should you need to. At 55 and above, you should have most of your major financial goals accomplished, and you should be nearing the completion of your base wealth goal of 12 times your pay.

A popular rule of thumb uses your age to calculate what percentage of your money you should have in bonds. The rule is based off of the fact that you are able to risk more in stocks as you are younger and that you want to gradually step away from it as you age – very similar to the ratio set forth by Farrell. The investing allocation (how you separate your investments) for the stock and bond mix is to subtract your age from 90 and invest that percentage in stocks. For example, at age 30, 60 percent of your money should be in stocks (because 90 minus 30 is 60). Because both methods achieve nearly the same result, it does not matter which one you use. It depends more on your risk tolerance and the discipline to change your allocation when your age changes. I personally prefer Farrell's rule, because it is more of an automatic system, one that I don't have to think about changing every year.

Paper Trading

Before you get into any investment, wouldn't it be great if you could simulate the stocks you would buy and see if you would have been successful or if you could test out some of the things you've heard in this book without risking your own cash? Well, you can. It's called paper trading. Paper trading is like practice for investors. Websites like Investopedia.com allow you to buy real stocks at real prices, but with fake money. Think of it as the Monopoly board game: the places may be real, but the money isn't.

Paper trading is another term for stock simulation. With paper trading, you get the benefit of experience and learning what to expect without risking your own cash. You can see for yourself how an index fund compares to buying individual stocks.

I suggest that everyone who does not have any experience with stocks try paper trading for one year prior to actually entering the market. You can learn some valuable lessons that will pay off when the real time comes.

Other Investment Options

Wall Street isn't the only place in which you can make your money grow. For some, it is the easiest to get into, but it is not for everyone. Some people prefer physical investments, There are advantages and disadvantages to both; the key is finding which strategy works for you and your situation. Here are a few other investing methods:

Property

Land is one of the only resources that cannot be replaced, renewed, or reproduced. There are thousands of people who have become wealthy through buying and selling properties, and with the right amount of money saved up, you, too, can jump into these types of investments. Again, like any investment it is not invincible; that was evident for many in 2008. If you were to buy a home to rent, what happens if the tenant decides not to pay? If you suddenly need to use a lot of money to pay for something, you can't just sell half the house, much less get the money from a house within a few days.

The selling process in real estate can take weeks, even months. These are concerns you will have to weigh, along with any maintenance and taxes. Despite these risks, buying property has the advantage of being insured, unlike stocks or bonds. This is one advantage that no other investment option has. I strongly suggest that you involve yourself in at least one investment in real estate, even if it's just your own home. Real estate is one of the largest generators of wealth and shouldn't be left off the table.

Franchising

Franchising gives you the option to own your own business with the support of a large name and product backing you. It is also one the best ways to start a company due to brand value. Instead of starting from the ground up, you can buy and sell what already exist. For example, McDonald's is a franchise. Why sell burgers from your kitchen and advertise by word of mouth when Mickey D's has done all the work for you? You also can receive training for your employees and tips to make your branch as successful as possible. Subway, Hampton Hotels, and Jiffy Lube are just a few companies with branches available to buy and launch on your own.

One major reason many people decide not to get into franchising is the start-up costs and franchising fees. Subway, for one, charges an ongoing fee of 8 percent royalty in addition to its initial $15,000 franchising fee. In many cases, this investment option is not cheap, but franchises can be very, very profitable.

They also have the advantage of being inherited easily and are much more in your control than stocks and sometimes property. You can be in charge of the hiring of employees; in some cases, you can choose whether to offer certain deals or products and the building location. When it comes to stocks, not only do you not control the market, but you cannot physically touch the investment. Franchising gives you the ability to do all of this with the support and backing of a well-known name and system.

Cars

I began my personal investing with used cars, and with the right network of people and start-up cash, you may find this venue profitable, as well. There are two main keys to this investing strategy, however: 1) It is imperative that you build a relationship with mechanics and car experts. Similar to investing in housing, unless you are a do-it-yourself person, you will need someone to check the car out and make any adjustments; 2) Find a well-qualified auction in your area, and do your research.

I became quite familiar with the Kelly Blue Book as a teenager, and it always paid off. Knowing the value of a used car, with the aid of a mechanic, has saved me thousands.

As with most selling, you may want to work backwards. It is best to know several people who need cars before you invest in getting one and fixing it up.

Without this, you may find yourself stocking up on cars without a consumer base of people who will buy. Depending on your mechanic connections and the auction you attend, you can get started with as low as $1000.

Micro-Lending

The field of micro lending is relatively young but can yield decent returns for people who are more conservative investors. Micro lending is the process of loaning small amounts of money, sometimes as low as $25, through an Internet mediator.

The person applying for the loan, however, will not be applying for a simple $25 loan but something much larger, usually for the purpose of paying off debts or starting their own company. If approved, applicants receive small amounts of money from different people. Over time, they pay your potion of the loan back, with interest, as if you were the bank.

One of the largest advantages of micro lending is that you are able to make a return on your money without risking much of your personal cash. Instead of loaning out $500, you can loan out only $50, while nine others fund the rest. The other advantage of this investing method is the ability to see the applicant's loan history. You have the ability to decide whether or not they are credit-worthy and see what exactly they'll be using the money for. The disadvantage, of course, is the possibility of your loan defaulting, which would mean that you would not get your portion of money back. The other disadvantage is that the returns probably are not large enough to make you wealthy; they do, however, provide a steady enough income to be more profitable than a savings account or money market fund. You can visit The Lending Club or Prosper websites to get more information.

Entrepreneurship

Explaining the advantages and drawbacks of entrepreneurship would take an entire book. Simply put, however, the majority of the millionaire population is self-employed in some right. This route may be the most risky and rewarding; when starting your own company, you have to risk your money along with your reputation. Failing, in some cases, could result in losing more than just your money, but the rewards can be spectacular. The founders of Google were entrepreneurs. Steve Jobs was an entrepreneur who began by selling computers from his garage. If you are committed to your vision and have a plan, perhaps investing in your entrepreneurial endeavors is for you.

Conclusion

Every type of investment has some risk attached to it; some types carry more risk than others. A completely risk-free investment is likely one without much profit. You will not be able to simply save your way to $1 million; you will need to grow your money in some way.

Listed above are just a few paths that many have taken to amass their fortunes. The best one(s) for you, however, should be based on your passion and professional background. That does not mean lock yourself into having only one way to make money; you should make yourself versatile and have multiple streams of income. Don't be afraid to branch out and learn a new field. To really make your money work for you is to fully employ one or more of these methods in your financial plan with confidence and commitment.

CHAPTER SIX

How Not to Fail

All plans are perfect until reality hits them. The sad part is that, in regard to your finances, the "reality" is that most people lack the discipline necessary to build wealth.

Recall that self-control was the second most important skill when it comes to becoming a millionaire; the first was being honest to all people.

Since self-control can't be grown or purchased overnight, you don't have the time or the money to waste to wait until you gain the right amount of self-control to build wealth.

Doing so is another surefire way to stay broke. We'll take each topic section of the book: savings, investing, and avoiding common money mistakes, and lay out a plan that will save you from yourself, making your wealth plan reality-proof.

We know that those who have more self-control and willpower are more likely to be successful in life and are more prepared to build wealth. Those who are not able to look long-term and plan ahead are more likely to fail.

So, what if this is not you? Are you doomed to a life of financial struggle? No, not as long as you take a few preventative measures.

The Power of Automation

To reach your savings goal, automation is the key to success. It will be nearly impossible NOT to reach your goal if you are automating your savings contributions. Though the term "automation" may seem like something complex, it is really quite simple. It means that you're saving your money without even seeing it first. It's very similar to an automatic cable bill payment. It comes right out of your account, and you'll never miss a payment.

Unlike other bills you may have to pay, there are times when you may forget to contribute to savings, pay yourself less than the bill amount, or decide not to pay yourself altogether. You cannot allow yourself to get in the way of your own savings.

The power of persuasion is crippling, especially when you are persuading yourself. Subconsciously, you persuade yourself all the time. Why didn't you go to the gym? Why did you take those few extra bites after you were full? Why did you buy something expensive when something more reasonable was attainable? These are all examples.

Automating your savings takes this variable out of the equation. You can't spend what you can't see, and that's why you cannot fail with this method.

The set-up for this process is very simple. You can go online to your bank account information and, under the transfer section, schedule a recurring payments to your savings. You may also be able to do this on your banking app, over the phone or in person at the bank.

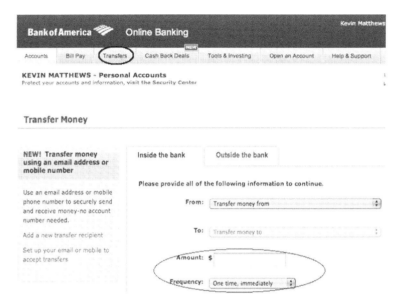

It is best to do this on pay day so that you pay yourself first. As an alternative, if you have direct deposit your employer you may be able automate your paycheck into your savings account for you. The advantage of going through the employer is that you can set it up as percentage; your paycheck can be allocated, without you being forced to calculate this amount each time you get paid and transfer the money over yourself. Though calling the HR department and getting in touch with the right people may be difficult, depending on your employer, it may be worth the effort. After all, you'll only have to do it once – that's the beauty of it.

You can also do this with your investments. Currently, as reported by CNN, one in every two Americans is not saving a dime for retirement – for many of the reasons that I've already spelled out. Lack of a long-term outlook and goal are at the top of the list. Also, because retirement is so far away, it seems as if there is plenty of time to make up any losses that may have occurred. Not only is that not the case, but it's the opposite. The longer you wait, the harder it is to catch up to what you will need to build wealth.

On the reverse side, the younger you start, the more wealth you can build. Many Americans' retirement contributions aren't automatic, there're problematic. Those who do save regularly for retirement normally have this goal on the back burner, and they contribute to it when they "have the money," or when it comes to mind. Either scenario will keep you from building wealth.

The key to building your retirement savings without fail is automation. It's the single best tool for building your wealth, and it can ensure that you and your goals won't crumble. Though automation is the single best method of savings, there are a few other techniques you can employ to save money and make a positive impact on your financial life. Bank of America has a "Keep the Change" program that rounds your purchases up to the nearest dollar and deposits the extra amount into your savings account. Wells Fargo and Chase also offer some version of this feature. You can check local credit unions, too, to see if they offer this or similar services; you might be surprised to learn of many advantages that smaller banks have over their larger, more well-known competitors.

Even if your bank does not have this option, you can always do it on your own. Make it a point not to spend your change; save it in one spot in your home. Having change spread out all over the house is not as motivating as seeing it pile up inside a large jar or 32-ounce cup. In money management, it is imperative to set goals, but it can be difficult to set a specific goal to save in change. Imagine someone saying, "I want to save $341.23 in change this year." It doesn't exactly work that way; the best way to go about it is to set goals with the item you save your change in. For example, if you have a small piggy bank, you can set a goal to fill it up 3 times per year. This makes your savings more measurable and motivating.

Though saving change can be effective, there are larger ways to get into the habit of saving money. One very effective technique is to get into the habit of collecting dollar bills. The best to collect are either $1s or $5s, but never both at the same time. (Collecting both $1s and $5s will likely require too much of your attention and will be too difficult to implement in the long run.) Focusing on one bill can add up to hundreds saved at the end of the year. Also, doing this will force you to use cash more often, which will help you budget more. This will require discipline, but will reward you with well-earned savings. I also suggest, again, having one place to build your collection such as a piggy bank or cup to keep you motivated.

As another motivation boost, you can use the money saved to pay for Christmas shopping or birthday shopping for yourself, provided that you only use the money that was saved to make purchases. Not all savings and discipline has to be used for future gains. There is nothing wrong with responsibly enjoying your money. Just remember the bill that you decide to save; you must keep it and collect it. You cannot spend it until the end of the year or until you've reached your date agreement.

Play Good Defense

In almost every arena, we are drawn to the offensive side of things. Slam dunks, last-second slap-shots, long putts for eagles, and Hail Marys excite us, move us, and cause the roar of millions. Not only are we obsessed with offense in the sports world, but we're also drawn to it when it comes to money, too. We love to find out who has the highest paycheck, what celebrity made the most last year, who's on the Forbes 50, which house is biggest on MTV Cribs – the list goes on. This is the offensive side of your money – how much you bring in and how much you show off.

What we too often forget is that there are two sides to every story, and even with your money, there is a heads and a tails. Just as in any game, from chess to football, a good defense is needed to pull off a victory. You can only build wealth if you have not only a decent offense but also a good defense. The better your defense, the larger your wealth. Imagine this scenario:

Your class reunion is coming up in a few months. Instead of going through a crash diet or dangerous weight loss pills, you decide to do the old-fashioned and reliable working out at the gym. You consult a doctor, who tells you that you'll need to exercise and burn at least 400 calories per day.

You head to the gym every day for weeks, and you successfully burn 400 calories every time. On the eve of the reunion, you weigh in, just to find out that you haven't lost any weight at all. What happened? You played great offense by working out consistently, but you forgot all about the defense. You worked out to burn the 400 calories, and you celebrated by eating those same 400 calories.

Playing defense is the act of retaining at least some of the effort that you've worked for. When it comes to your money, a bad defense can be illustrated, just as it is in your workout. You may be great at getting a large income and great at spending it, and if that's the case, that's why you're broke. Both sides of your money, offense and defense, have two portions. The offense consists of your income and spending, and the defense is made up of budgeting and saving. You want to be a person who plays both well; becoming too heavily invested in one aspect can be very damaging.

Focus on defense too much, and you'll struggle to enjoy the money you have. Though defense is good, and it is impossible to build wealth without it, it's absolutely possible to have "too much of a good thing." The obsession with the concept of saving can lead to a miser's mentality.

Those who brag about living off of $300 less per month might fall into this boat. Saving is important, but that's no way to live. An extreme indulgence in the defensive side of your money can lead you on a cheapskate path, and oftentimes, there is no need to live to the extreme.

Focusing too much on offense, as we've discussed, can be a major pitfall, too. If all of your attention is invested in making money and spending money, how much will you have left at the end? Absolutely nothing. As alluring as the offense is when it comes to money, you'll have to tailor it back some and make room for some solid defense. The only way to build wealth is to have balance: a good money-making strategy *and* a good budgeting and savings strategy.

The "Well, Too Late Now" Complex

You likely don't need to be coached on how to spend your money, but when it comes to budgeting and savings, good advice isn't always easily within reach. If you're automating to save 12 percent of your income, you've already won half of the battle. The other half of a good defensive strategy comes from budgeting, which was discussed earlier.

But even with a strong budget that follows all of the rules, the temptation to overspend will always be there, and once a budget is broken, it is much harder to stay focused and not continue to break the bank. This comes from what I call the "Well, Too Late Now" complex.

I see it in some of my students and clients. When a goal or desired result is obviously not achieved, the person doesn't work to get closer to the goal, but instead ensures that the goal will never be reached.

In my math classes, I occasionally have students race to complete a set of basic math problems for a warm-up. The winner becomes the world record holder. Once a student finishes first, others sometimes find it hopeless to continue and give up all hope in finishing, even though finishing the drill will help them in the long run – not to mention that the first finisher might have made a mistake! This also happens in dieting and with your money.

When you find that you've overspent by a few dollars, this complex can kick in as you think, "Well it's too late now; I'm already over my budget. I might as well go ahead and treat everyone to lunch now, too." While your complex may not be as generous as others', psychologically, it still occurs and can ruin your financial goals. You have to be patient, stay the course, and make adjustments in your budget to make the best of what you have left … and lastly, learn from your mistakes, and don't make it a habit to overspend.

Be an Informed Shopper

As with most issues, it's much more conducive to avoid bad habits than to repair them. Remember that budgets don't break themselves; they break when we underestimate or overspend.

The problem is that, even though we may have good intentions, advertisers and companies have gotten awfully good at getting you to spend money, even though you know you don't need to.

They spend enormous amounts of time trying to separate you from your money. The things that you pay attention to least when you're shopping could end up costing you the most. Many stores, especially those in the mall, attempt to hook you not only with their bright sales posters and fancy displays, but also by marketing to every one of your five senses. Some stores pay very close attention to how their store smells. This, in addition to the lighting of a store, can make you feel more comfortable and at home, making you want to relax and spend more time in the store.

The more time in the store, the more likely you are to become a paying customer. It's a marketing rule of thumb that buyers pay more attention to the music and sound of the store than how it smells, so retailers are very conscious of their playlists, as well. In 2010, CNN reported that playing Christmas music can keep people in a store up to 30-40 percent longer[20].

A company's objective is to make you spend as much as possible, and as a person who is trying to build wealth and play good defense, your job is to buy only what you came for,

---

[20]   Bragg, J. (2012, November 22). How stores get you to spend more. *CNNMoney.*

which, in the moment, can seem impossible. Here are some ways to avoid spending more than you intended:

#1 Shop alone

Try to shop alone at all costs. Your kids and friends can subconsciously pressure you to spend way more than you intended. Shopping with kids is an obvious obstacle; they can grab hold of things, throw fits, and persuade you to buy things that you know you don't need. Because you won't always be able to drop the kids off for a grocery store run, you should run over the list with your kids and allow them to take a bit of responsibility in getting those groceries.

For example, let them hold the shopping list (which you should never travel without) and tell you what needs to be purchased. This will teach them responsibility and how to plan ahead, and it may also be fun. By having your kids focus on the list, they'll be less likely to venture off or pout their way into your buying things that you don't need.

When it comes to shopping with friends, it's a different story. This is probably more dangerous than shopping with your children. Shopping with your friends can trigger a serious subconscious effect. When you throw friends into the mix, shopping is no longer a task; it becomes a social event. Here are a few words to the wise: social events and shopping should never be mixed, and "retail therapy" should be eradicated from your vocabulary.

The fact that friends can affect your finances was evident in a recent study that suggests Facebook can make you both fat and poor[21]. This is because being around friends can increase your

---

[21]   Mielach, D. (2012, December 12). Can Facebook Make You Fat and Poor? *BusinessNewsDaily.com.*

self-esteem, which negatively impacts your decision-making skills and judgment. If a website that exposes you to thousands of your friends can do that without them being in the store with you, imagine what could happen if they ride, walk, and shop with you. Of course, there is nothing wrong with self-esteem, but when it comes to shopping in particular, it may not be the best. When you could have been going into a store to buy just one dress, your friends can suggest that a few others on the sale rack go well with another pair of shoes that you already own.

Of course, your friends don't suggest bad financial choices for you on purpose, but it's best if you go it alone. Additionally, when you're with friends, you can feel pressure to buy. You certainly don't want to be the one who goes through all the stores without a shopping bag. This can force you to waste money on something you may not even use or need just to fit in. Also, if you're taking your friends with you, you may feel pressure to buy so that it does not feel like you're dragging them across town for nothing. This is perhaps one of the most underrated ways to waste money; avoid it and play good defense by shopping alone.

#2 *Look, but don't touch*

Recall that stores already try to employ your five senses against you; don't do more damage to yourself. When you begin to touch items, whether it's clothes or gadgets or books, the more you interact with them, the more connected you feel.

Once you connect with that item and you do not buy it, you feel as if you're missing out on something, that having that item will somehow make your life much easier. You're actually 22 percent more likely to buy just because you touched an item, according to Martin Lindstrom, author of *Biology: Truth and Lies About Why We Buy.*

Think about how the Apple store is designed: everything is well-lit, there is normally music playing which no doubt was selected on purpose, and everything at the store is right at waist level – just high enough for you to touch everything in the store. It's no wonder so many people feel connected to their iPhones and that there has been such a shift since their creation. Never have there been communities of people who bonded over having the same type of phone before. At times, iPhone users seem like members of a fraternity or sorority. And to squelch any feelings of being left out, millions of people each year subscribe to the belief that they, too, must have this hot, new item to become members of the club.

In short, though it will not be possible for every shopping situation, make it a point not to get too attached to any item – literally.

#3 Don't worry about being an early adopter

It rarely pays to be an early adopter of technology. In fact, it usually costs you more. Not only are first generation items generally flawed in some capacity, but there are usually cheaper versions and generic versions that will be introduced and lower the cost of the original.

Going back to the iPhone, in 2007, when it was introduced, it cost $600. If you were one of the first people to have it, you may have been considered cool at the moment, but you were probably considered dumb about a year later. Though phones could record video at that point, the original iPhone did not, and of course, without fail, the next generation iPhone had added that capacity. What's worse is that the price dropped significantly. Now, an iPhone 5 with some companies is free, while the iPhone 5c (who knows which version they'll have come out with when you're reading this) is $199 dollars, cheaper than the original and considerably better.

Similar findings occurred with the PlayStation consoles and the Amazon Kindle. Be patient, and wait for prices to become more reasonable before you make a technology purchase. A good defense is predicated upon patience.

#4 Always shop with a list. Always.

One of my father's bits of wisdom he would share with my brother and me was, "Boys, if you don't have a plan, you will become a part of someone else's." He was right, and it applies to much more than I ever anticipated. Anytime you go shopping without a list, whether it be groceries or clothes, you don't have a plan. And when you don't have a plan, the retailer certainly has one lined up for you – one that includes you spending more time and more money than you'd likely be comfortable with.

Making a shopping list prior to your trip is vital, as it serves two purposes. The first is to save money. Stores rely on you forgetting items and being an impulsive shopper. At Wal-Mart, for example, all of the smaller items like gum, candy, lint rollers, and magazines are all at the checkout. They are counting on you saying, "Oh, yeah … I do want to see how Oprah came up with that idea," and, "Nothing better than a Snickers to go along with my reading; I've earned it."

Once you start to question yourself, you've become part of their plan. The only question that you should be asking yourself is, "Is it on the list?" If it's not, then you clearly have your answer.

The second reason to never shop without a list is the time factor. Usually, the longer you are in a store, the more you will spend, and retailers know that. Time is and will always be your biggest asset, not money. Therefore, you cannot afford to waste time wandering around the store, aimlessly waiting for an idea of what you need to buy to pop into your head. With a list, you can get in, get out, and get on your way.

Invest In Yourself

Society has done a good job at telling us what we can and cannot do. As a result, many people, probably even you, have earned some money doing things that don't really fit the description of your "dream job."

Too many people pass up their talents to do something that will simply make money, or they are persuaded out of their original major in college to pursue something more profitable. If you are a current college student, should you drop out your senior year and follow your life passion for origami? Probably not...but you shouldn't let go of that dream completely, either.

Do what is necessary to secure a living, and always have a backup plan. If you always wanted to be a celebrity real estate agent and actor but ended up in accounting, definitely keep your job for the moment. The key is to continue investing in yourself to move toward your ultimate goal. I do not believe that you are truly wealthy until you are able to do what you were born to do. And to get to that point, you must invest in yourself; no one will do it for you.

When you follow your passion instead of a paycheck, that's when you become wealthy. Entrepreneurs realize this, especially those who do what they love each and every day. To get to that point, make an investment in your own interests and hobbies.

My passion is to get thousands of people to build their own wealth, to take their 9-to-5 job, whether it be at Wal-Mart or on Wall Street, and make that money last. Too often, when looking at others, we only see the results, not the work or the investment that those people made on a night-in, night-out basis to get there.

From playing basketball to writing books, you have to invest in yourself to achieve your dream. The very first personal finance book I read was *The Automatic Millionaire* by David Bach.

During spring break of my freshman year of undergrad, I became excited as I learned how to create wealth for myself, and I knew, at that point, that I wanted to give that joy to others. The way I saw it, I had two choices: I could have let my dream wither away, or I could chase after it.

My sophomore year, I began investing in myself. I read constantly, sometimes finishing up to seven books in a week. In 2010, during an internship in New York, I focused on starting my own company and began doing research on starting a business in college; by September of that same year, all of my investment – not just in money, but in time and energy – paid off when it was incorporated.

Investing in yourself is taking the time to continue those hobbies that you enjoy and taking classes in the things that you are interested in.

Not only will spending time in a way that you value and enjoy help you become less stressed, but it could also be an avenue to additional income.

Investing in yourself isn't always something related to a hobby; it could be getting an advanced degree or just finishing school. It's all about getting better and improving on things that you need and want. If you think that your learning and growing ended with college or high school, you were mistaken.

The time and money you invest in classes, books, and trainings will have a profound impact on how you feel and your earning potential down the line. I have probably spent thousands on books from Barnes and Noble, Amazon, and people off the street just in the last two years alone, but look at the results: I've been able to produce multiple books and seminars from the skills I have learned, and I've improved my craft because of it.

Imagine what would happen if you began fueling your fire. Some people dream; others wake up and chase their dreams. Which path will you choose?

Question Yourself

Another way to invest in you is to ask yourself the right questions. When things don't work out the way you planned, instead of thinking, "Why did this go wrong?" or, "Why does this happen to me?" you should be thinking, "How can I make this better next time?" These are empowering questions, ones that get you thinking about solutions and responsibility. It's the difference between asking yourself or someone else, "Why am I always broke?" and, "How can I start saving my money?" The former focuses on the root or the cause, but it is not a solution. The latter will most likely be answered with a strategy or method to actually get you to change your behavior.

If you are wondering what you should be investing in when it comes to yourself, refer to the SEE exercise in chapter 4. If those are the most important things to you, then invest in those things! You can also further question yourself to find your passion and begin pursuing it. Here are some good questions to get you started:

If you knew you could not fail, what would you do?

If you had to work just one job, every day, nonstop, what would it be?

How can your hobbies or interests make you money?

What things do you have to do to move toward your dream job or lifestyle?

Why is that dream job/lifestyle so important to you?

What can you do on a daily basis to achieve that dream?

The final question is not only my favorite but perhaps the most important. No matter how strong your passion is, it will likely not be realized in one day. It will take tiny – not small, but *minuscule* steps each and every day to reach it.

This book is a result of daily tiny steps. There came a time that I was so busy with my first teaching job that I could only afford to read and research 10 pages per day. That was it. But every month, there was another book that I had completed and added to my library. You should now have a good starting point for what and how to invest in yourself for wealth and decrease your stress.

Also note that many millionaires are entrepreneurs and have grown their wealth so because of their passions and their daily commitment to improving themselves. If you're thinking to yourself that you don't have the time to dedicate daily to your dream, then it's no wonder you are not moving toward it.

Even if it's five minutes a day, take one small step to invest in yourself, and benefits will come, slowly, but surely, as a result.

What Time Zone Are You In?

I hinted earlier that delayed gratification was a huge factor in creating wealth. It's because becoming wealthy will not happen overnight; anyone that promises you that is lying. There are no true, reliable ways to get rich quickly. Even professional sports, besides providing rather shaky long-term wealth plans, are not instant solutions; it takes years of practice to get to that level of athleticism. Building your fortune will be no different.

While there are ways to legitimately boost the speed of your progress, there is no 1-, 5-, or even 7-year plan to make millions. Saving your money and investing, the most reliable way to build wealth, could take up to 40 years. Do you think you can stay focused for that long?

One major difference between those who have a millionaire mindset and those who have a poverty mindset are in the "time zones" in which they think. You have a choice to think day to day, week to week, month to month, year to year, or decade to decade. The farther out you think, the more successful you are likely to become.

The poverty mindset is a present mindset; it relates to one who only thinks of today and does not worry about tomorrow. Those with this mindset do not believe in saving or investing, only spending and using every cent for pleasure purposes. This mindset is poisonous and prevailing in today's society.

The ubiquitous phrase, "YOLO" (You Only Live Once) is a testament to that very mentality. Other supporters of this thought process are quick to call out another familiar phrase, "You can't take it with ya' when you're gone."

While both may be true, they are two beliefs that can hinder you in building wealth. Yes, you do only live once, so why not make the most of your money and be able to relax instead of stress about how your bills are going to get paid? And yes, you cannot take your worldly wealth with you when you're gone, but you can leave it behind to take care of others. Wealth is about giving just as much as it is about accumulating.

Being wasteful is not only stupid but also selfish. Wealthy, long-term thinkers attempt to take care of their loved ones even after they pass by providing scholarship funds and eliminating debt that their loved ones would have had to pay off.

With this poverty mindset, there is a paradox that can prevent many people from thinking beyond their current situation. If you are starving today, how can you think about eating next week? It's like telling a student who has been known to fail classes that they should begin saving for college, when even graduating from the eighth grade seems to be a tremendous feat.

Though these immediate roadblocks may seem daunting, you should never be limited in your ability to think beyond the current moment in time. By reading this book, you have already shown that you can look further than what's right in front of you.

Those with the wealthy mindset, on the other hand, are those who plan ahead and take daily actions that are aligned to long-term goals. When it comes to planning, sometimes, their goals are years in advance.

Nothing during the day-to-day stress will distract them from what they ultimately want to achieve, even outside of wealth. Remember that true wealth encompasses more than just money; it's the ability and freedom to pursue your desires. You can have a large sum of money, but if you are so tied down to your profession that you cannot enjoy time with family and friends, that is not real wealth – that is slavery with a large paycheck. The goal of wealth is to be able to have both, without the worries of going broke or needing to work for the rest of your life. And to reach that point, you have to plan ahead.

To become wealthy, you will need these two ingredients: a plan and patience. At this point in the book, you have already received a solid plan as to how to define and achieve your monetary wealth goal. But what about patience? How do you control something that is so abstract? Part of the answer comes from your responses to the questions in the last section (investing in yourself).

Another portion comes from modeling yourself after millionaires so that you are very deliberate in how you spend and not so weak-minded to fall into the traps of the hottest trends and Money Lies. Lastly, you can become more patient and successful by changing your time zone. And to do that, you will need to take a look at how you set and monitor your financial and personal goals.

Wealth and Willpower

Roy Baumeister and John Tierney, authors of *Willpower: Rediscovering the Greatest Human Strength*, have a mountain of evidence suggesting that willpower alone is the greatest trait that will predict success, from wealth to dieting to grades. Specifically, when it comes to building wealth, they were spot on: willpower, or being self-disciplined, is one of the biggest factors in your ability to create wealth for yourself. After all, you will have to have a great deal of self-control to curtail a large spending habit or cut off a financial addiction that is making you broke. Millionaires agree with these findings, too: remember that, in the list of traits that millionaires believe led to their financial success, "being well-disciplined" was tied for first with "being honest with all people."

Planning and patience go hand in hand. The experiment recorded by Roy and John explains:

> Researchers monitored college students taking part in a program to improve their skills at studying, in addition to receiving the usual instruction on how to use time efficiently. The students were randomly assigned three planning coordinators. One group was told to make daily plans for what, when, and where to study. Another made similar plans only month to month instead of day to day, and the third did not make plans at all.

Which group do you think performed better? If you thought the daily planners, you're in line with what the researchers thought would work best, but you were both wrong.

The monthly planning group did the best. Even a year after the program ended, the monthly planners were still getting better grades than the daily planners – most of whom by this point had largely abandoned planning, daily or otherwise.

Why didn't daily planning work? First, it's time-consuming. It is much harder to make thirty daily plans instead of one monthly plan. Because daily planners have the ability to know exactly what they should be doing at each moment, yet there is no such thing as a perfect schedule (as things nearly always fall off by a few minutes), they would get discouraged and give in. If there is lots of traffic, you get tied up on the phone, or you're just running late, the whole day and daily plan could be knocked off, whereas, with a monthly plan, you are able to make small adjustments with much less stress and still accomplish your goal.

This is the same reason that we have monthly budgets instead of daily or weekly budgets, and it's also why I advocate for having play money in your budget. Without it, you'll be budgeting every single dollar and cent, and that will be stressful. Miscalculate by a dollar, and your whole budget is blown.

Additionally, you can see the differences between mindsets of wealthy thinkers and poor thinkers. Thinking day to day is ineffective and stressful, while having a larger outlook can improve your flexibility and focus. When you're looking at a detailed, daily budget, it's too easy to be distracted. Just as day-to-day investors panic about stock prices and daily changes in the market while index, long-term investors aren't even concerned with minute-to-minute updates, when you change your time zone, you become more patient. When you become more patient, you will be able to weather the day-to-day distractions that could separate you from the road to wealth.

Conclusion

To master the world of money is to first master your mind. Take as much out of the equation as possible by automating your savings and any regular expenses. By knowing the psychological pitfalls, you can avoid overspending, as well.

There is a difference between a calling and a career; to realize your full potential, you will need to fully invest in yourself in some capacity. For some, it could mean saving enough money to launch their own business; for others, it could mean just traveling with their children. What good is accumulating wealth if you are not able to use it for the things that you were born to do? Being financially stable should be about living out those dreams without risking your assets or going broke to do it. Will you be bold enough to follow a proven plan to build financial strength or let the worries and doubts of others leave you weak?

CHAPTER SEVEN

Keeping it Simple

To ensure your financial success, you need to keep things simple. That's why I have opted out of including complicated formulas, graphs, and metrics in this book. The simpler your plan, the more likely you are to accomplish your goal.

For this reason, I strongly urge you to refer back to the savings ratios and the wealth definition charts in chapter 4. These will keep your goals simple and clear, no matter what your pay may be. If you take nothing else from this book, know that simplicity is your friend. For too long, much of the personal finance industry has been defined by complexity and confusion. It does not have to be that way.

As long as you can numerically define your own wealth (which you can do with my chart) and have a solid plan to reach it (your savings ratio and index funds), you will be able to reach your destination. Finance has the ability to look like complex calculus, but in essence, it is not. Don't let others persuade you into thinking that an option or plan that looks more sophisticated is more reliable. When you fall into this trap, you begin to fall into the entertainment and flashiness factor when it comes to your money – and that's not needed.

Let's be honest. The plan that I have laid out for you in this book is not extravagant. It is not laced with an untouchable vocabulary, and it did not take a lawyer to read and explain. It is plain, simple, and to the point, no flashiness needed. My plan reflects the lives of many millionaires today: plain, simple, and not flashy – the way it should be. There is no need to consistently worry about your stock choices or your financial position each and every week. Those who do are often less successful when it comes to investing.

Let's compare two people, John and Brandon. John graduated with a finance degree from a very prestigious university and now works in the finance department for a Silicon Valley tech giant. Because his background and profession are in finance, he makes his own decisions when it comes to investing. He gets emails and text alerts when stocks rise and fall. He's able to make trades from his cell phone, computer, and tablet. John is always connected to his investments and does everything to ensure their success.

Brandon, on the other hand, is a lazy investor. He's put half of his money in an index fund and the other half in boring government bonds. Brandon graduated with an English degree from a small college and considers himself very math-averse. Brandon only checks his investments twice a year, at most, but he never makes any adjustments.

If each continues his habits, which do you think would be better off financially in 20-30 years? The answer would be Brandon, by a long shot. But why would someone who puts such little work in be more successful than someone whose background and profession is in finance? The answer is twofold.

The first reason why John would not do as well as Brandon is overconfidence. This can happen whether or not you majored in finance. When it comes to money, overconfidence can be a serious issue. Because so much pride can be tied up with money, we can be very reluctant to seek help or guidance. Additionally, the more math savvy you may be, the less likely you are to admit that you could be overstating your own ability.

Second, checking your financial status each and every day actually hurts you. A recent survey by *Money Magazine* found that 22 percent of investors say they look up the prices of their investments every day and 49 percent check on them at least once a week. The author of *Your Money, Your Brain*, Jason Ziwieg, says, "After all, time is money – but money is also time. If you are compulsively checking up on the prices of your investments, you're not only hurting your financial returns, you're unnecessarily taking precious time away from the rest of your life."[22] Investing and building wealth should be long-term endeavors. Constantly changing your investments can be an extremely bad idea, not only because it's more expensive to constantly change investments due to transaction fees, but also because, psychologically, we're so sensitive to short-term losses. To better tame those impulses, it is suggested to only monitor your investments four times a year, either at the end of each calendar quarter or on four other dates that are equidistant.

You will have no need to follow the market's daily movements, largely because you are a long-term investor who isn't concerned with day-to-day happenings, also because

22   Zweig, J. (2007). Your money and your brain: how the new science of neuroeconomics can help make you rich. New York: Simon & Schuster.

you are an index investor who isn't worried about a single company's success or failure (because you own them all). You're keeping your investment life simple by avoiding the Wall Street guessing game about which company will make the most money overnight. It's one large but singular and simple focus.

Keep Your Emotions and Habits in Check

Money is and will always be an inanimate object. It's a medium of exchange to which we, as a society, have agreed to assign value. Money is actually nothing more than that; however, our emotions have made money's meaning go well beyond its intended function. People have fought over money, made rash decisions over money, and ended lives, all for a few pieces of paper. If your only goal is to become wealthy for the sake of becoming wealthy, you will never reach it, because no amount will ever satisfy your emotional need to collect and hoard riches. This is not the way to live.

Your emotions can not only drive you into ruin with your finances, but they can also drive you to success. Building wealth can be born out of the need to send your children to college or pass down the family business. Your emotions and self-control can dictate how successful you will be when it comes to building wealth. There are a few things that you can do to avoid falling into an emotional and financial trap.

Consider this point, another from Zweig: "How much money you make is less important than how much money you want – and how you spend it … no matter how much or little money you have, you can use it to lead a happier life if you under-stand the limits of what it can do for you and the power you can exert over it with self-control."

It's not about how much you make, but how your goals are defined and how you use your money to attain it. You must always be in control of your money; you must manage it, because if not, it will certainly manage you –from your emotions to your stress level. When you boil it all down, money buys you options; the more money you have, the more choices that are at your disposal.

The beauty of wealth is that the amount that you will ultimately have depends not on how much you have, but how much you manage what you have. When you fail to manage your money properly, you subject yourself to playing the victim role. Victims, in a financial sense, are prisoners of the moment and have very little control or interest in changing their situation. It's a dangerous mindset that can only be cured when one sees the power of thinking beyond their current financial time zone. If you can get your mind right, the money will follow.

Putting It All Together

Wealth is a full circle initiative. It begins with setting your mind up for success by eliminating all of the mental roadblocks and distractions and ends with a clear and simple plan for achieving your goal. By completing the reading of this book, you've now gained the full ability to do just that. Wealth is about doing a few small things exceptionally well. You don't have to be an expert or a math genius to get there. Above all, know that money does only what you tell it to. You have the power to switch jobs, start your own company, or get the necessary certifications to receive a higher paycheck. How you spend and save your money will determine how you can ultimately make more of it.

The decision to start this journey will require you to be responsible for yourself. From this point forward, you shouldn't blame your financial issues on money alone. The money doesn't spend itself; *you* spend *it*. You have the choice to either spend it on things that will build wealth or waste it on things that don't add value to your life in the long run. Money does not make those decisions for you. Making better financial decisions will require you to take a look at your motivations and habits; these will explain the pressures and impulses that may lure you into ill-advised purchases.

Peer pressure and society can often force us into positions that are not conducive to building wealth. It's why the Paycheck, Greed, Spending, and Reality TV Lies are so prevalent in our everyday financial habits.

Before you can even attempt to fix your finances, you must always begin with fixing yourself. What are the things that are inherently driving you to – or weighing you down and making it more difficult to – reach your full potential? Now that we've unveiled them, we must install strong values and beliefs that will not only help you build wealth, but also create a better, more comfortable life, from your finances to your family.

In June 2009, Investopedia contributor Stephanie Powers wrote an article detailing six traits that millionaires have that the rest of us can adopt. Three of them are based on a mindset for success. If the money lies are impediments that trick us into making others rich, what are some truths or values that we can adopt that will push you forward financially?

1) Think Independently

Taking control of your money will require you to think independently. You cannot allow the opinions, fears, or expectations of others dictate how you go about accomplishing your goals. You cannot compare or compete with others. When you lose this independent mindset, you begin to live above your means and adopt the money lies that drag you down. When everyone else has graduated college and bought brand new cars directly afterward, it takes an independent-minded person not to fall for those things, be content with building wealth over the long term, and not attempt to compare themselves to or one-up their peers.

Independent thinkers are not wrapped up in what others think or do. They are more concerned with where they are going and how they are going to get there. Recall that the number one car driven by millionaires is a Ford F-150. They're the most financially successful people in the United States, and they choose to drive that vehicle. Not a Bentley, Mercedes, or even a Lexus – but a Ford. They do this because they're not caught up in impressing others or meeting society's standards of what rich looks like.

They could care less what other people think rich looks like, because they know, for a fact, what wealth feels like. That is an independent mindset focused on specific goals, not persuaded by the beliefs and norms of others. Without this, it will be nearly impossible to build true wealth. Perhaps you will amass a large sum of money, but it will be just for the sake of having it and impressing others; a slave who works for attention, gratification, and greed is still a slave.

2) Creating Wealth Requires Vision

Having vision is having the ability to look beyond your current financial time zone. It's seeing past your struggles today and having the ability to prepare and plan, though you may not have the means to complete your vision at that very moment. It takes practice and patience, and you can only do so if you have a vision to which you can cling. You cannot be patient for something that you do not wish to happen, and you cannot practice and budget for a goal you have not set. Defining your wealth numerically is part of that vision. With it, you know exactly how much you need and how much further you have to go. Without it clearly defined, what reason would you have to save? Why would you budget? Those who cannot define what wealth is for themselves are doomed to never reach it.

Think of vision- and goal-setting on a broader scale. If you have no clue what your end goal is, how can you align your daily actions to ensure that whatever "it" is happens? The short answer is to depend on luck, which is why those who can least afford to gamble do it most. Lotto players are rarely well-off people who have solid financial goals and a plan to get there.

More than likely, they are people without a plan who are praying for a break. So then, if they reach it, their money is more than likely squandered just a few years later. If you don't have a strong vision for yourself, you can't take steps to reach your goals. And if you can't take steps to reach your goals, you'll never reach them. It's plain and simple.

3) Follow What You Love; Invest in Yourself

"Money is a byproduct of something I like to do very much."

—WARREN BUFFETT

When you aren't an independent thinker, you tend to fall prey to the idea that what you love or what you're passionate in will never make enough money to make a viable living. That is not the case, especially when you have a vision for following your passion. The reason why that old belief persists is that the previous two mindsets are not always present for those who want to passionately pursue their dreams.

Too often, those who are willing to go out on a limb and follow their passions do so on a whim. They'll drop out of college or high school to chase their dream of becoming an actor or dancer, ultimately to fail. Because this story is all too popular, we too often pigeonhole ourselves into "good jobs" that give us good pay but require little to no passion. You feel trapped on a career path that has nothing to do with the things you actually love. That is not true wealth.

Do what you love, and love what you do. That does not mean walk out of the job that keeps the bills paid and food on the table tomorrow morning. Many people assume that when you follow your dreams, you have to simply take a stand instantly. That's not the case. If you know what you love to do and want to make a living doing it, by all means, you should follow that path – but do so in a patient and planned manor. Don't risk your current status and security for a shaky and uncertain future.

To help ensure your success, again, you must set forth a strong vision for what and where you want to be and outline all the steps it will take to get there. In time, you can inch toward your goal and ease into a position where you will flourish. Without a solid plan for making the transition, you may feel that you're trapped and won't be able to go back to school or take that time off. The strongest visions have three aspects: the present, the end, and the in-between. The in-between is too often overlooked and under-planned. This is why many who decide to suddenly follow their dreams fall flat on their faces.

You need to plan each and every small step it takes, all the way from your current situation to your dream job or position. As a teacher, I had to use this concept in my lesson planning. If my students were to learn how to multiply fractions, I had to know how well they could multiply and divide whole numbers. I had to know if they knew what fractions were and if they could reduce them. I had to cover mixed numbers and improper fractions. These are all the things that go into the goal of multiplying fractions; without one of those in-between steps, my students could have easily gotten lost.

If you're majoring in something just to get a job or you are already working in a job that you know you are not passionate about, don't quit immediately. However, do immediately begin setting up the in-between steps it will take to properly transition from where you are to where you ultimately want to be. Those steps could range from attending classes on the weekends, going for a higher degree, or even dedicating yourself to a craft in your spare time until you have a large enough following to stand on your own.

Always remember that it takes time and that, as long as you have a strong vision and independent mindset, you will be heading in the right direction. "The average millionaire doesn't find his or her dream job until age 45 and tends to be 54, on average, before becoming a millionaire."[23] It's also been found that millionaires tried an average of 17 ventures before they were successful[24]. Only a strong vision and passion will

---

[23]   Powers, S. (2009, June 23). 6 Millionaire Traits That You Can Adopt. *Yahoo Finance.*

[24]   Powers, S. (2009, June 23). 6 Millionaire Traits That You Can Adopt. *Yahoo Finance.*

drive you to keep trying when conditions aren't perfect. Do what you love, follow your purpose, and wealth will follow.

There is a difference between a career and a calling, and to realize your full potential, you should invest and capitalize on the latter. The best creators of wealth have learned to maximize their inborn strengths, talents, and interests. What would have happened if Steve Jobs wasn't obsessed enough with his own creations and took the safe route of working for a computer repair store instead? What if Oprah just decided to stay in the comfort of television as a reporter instead of venturing to own her own production company, magazine, and TV network? Those who never achieve wealth and happiness will attempt to curb your thinking, telling you that your dreams are just fantasies or that job security is the best thing in the world to have at your side.

And then there's you – you cosign on their comments, suggesting that you cannot follow that passion because you cannot monetize it or that you're not even sure of what it is. I was that person once. I had to tune out all of the noise to find out what my calling was and what I was born to do. Your life, your voice, and your energy will only occur once on this planet. There will never be another you, and when you do what you were created to do, nothing can stop you.

I realized this in my second year of college. I didn't have a job and couldn't have a car on campus, and I was tired of being a broke college student. While this was a badge of honor for some and an excuse to beg for a free, home-cooked meal for others; I wasn't happy. Unsure of what unique skills I possessed, I had to dig deep into my own history and experience to find it.

For the majority of my childhood, my mother worked at a bank, and it was the very first place I was brought to from the hospital. I can't be sure if that's the sole reason I am who I am today, but I do believe that everything happens for a reason. As a kid, I loved calendars and planners and would make schedules of what video games to play and when, how much they would cost, and how much of my allowance and lunch money I could save to get the ones I wanted. In elementary school, I loved to play with expired checks that a lady at church gave me.

Upon graduating from college, I could have become a CPA, attended law school, or gone directly to Wall Street. I could have silenced my history and my unique interests to gain a comfortable paycheck from a white collar industry. I had two choices: to make someone else's dream come true or to follow my own path.

I had to go back to being a kid and figure out how to monetize the things that I'd do for free. I loved learning about money and budgeting, so I began to build a library of personal finance books. I got certified as a wealth coach and built a network of financial bloggers and authors.

None of these happened overnight but I am as happy now, as a speaker and author, as I was when I started, with a dollar and a dream. A lot of people are afraid of failure, but you can never truly fail when following your own path.

"All men dream: but not equally. Those who dream by night in the dusty recesses of their minds wake in the day to find that it was vanity: but the dreamers of the day are dangerous men, for they may act their dreams with open eyes, to make it possible."

—T.E. LAWRENCE

Final Thoughts

All the books, all the seminars, and all the advice in the world won't help you build wealth if you don't have a strong enough mental motivation to achieve it; that's why I've dedicated so much to the topics of the Money Lies and how today's wealthy truly live. But as we know, a mindset and ideal are nearly worthless without a plan to follow and guide you to your goal. I think that building wealth should be an opportunity that everyone has. It should not require a finance degree to understand how to achieve a comfortable amount of wealth and security. My wealth plan is simple and achievable for anyone, regardless of pay scale. My message can be summed up in five short points:

1   Acquire the Millionaire's Mind: avoid the distractions of what society *thinks* wealth looks like.
2   Build an emergency fund that is *at least* equal to three months of your expenses
3   Save 12-15 percent of your income for your retirement.
4   Eliminate debt.
5   Invest in yourself and your skills

Acknowledgements

This is always my favorite part of the book. Without it, not only would these words not be in front of you today, but I would not have the passion, love, and excitement that I have for inspiring others to build wealth.

First, to my grandfather, Reginald Watson: on October 27, 2012, just two days before my twenty-third birthday, you left us for a better place.

Two weeks earlier, I'd had the chance to see you for the last time before you passed. By then, it may have been too late; you may not have even remembered my name then, but I will always remember you. As much as I wanted to be with you as you read this book, I know that I cannot. But I know that you are looking down now, without Alzheimer's and without pain – know that your legacy will always live on.

To my parents: I thank you for instilling in me the values of hard work and granting me an allowance at the tender age of 8. It taught me the budgeting skills that grew into the passion and profession I have today. Who knew that two dollars a week could have amounted to so much down the line?

I also cannot forget to mention your support for me attending college so far from home. I know it wasn't always the easiest thing to do, especially with me missing holidays and summers, but without that support, I am certain that I would not have been able to come as far as I have or to go as far as I plan to without it.

To Kennedy, my baby sister: you're next, little girl! Go make history. To my little brother: I am proud of you. I've seen you grow through the toughest circumstances, and I know, with certainty, that nothing can stop you.

Much of my influence is a direct result of the history of the city to which I was born and raised: Tulsa, Oklahoma. Thank you to Dr. Marshall and Mr. Craig: before I even knew what my ultimate dreams were, you were always supportive of my ideas and leadership. Each of you have been a very strong influence on me as a man, educator, and entrepreneur.

There was a time in the summer of 2013 when I was ready to quit. I didn't ace the interview for the job I wanted, and this book wasn't where I wanted it to be. I sent an email out blindly, hoping that someone could inspire me and show me what and where to go with my career. It was Dr. Dennis Kimbro who replied, simply, "Call me," just days before Tiffany Aliche took the time to email me everything I needed to know about staying on track and marketing myself. I am forever grateful for their words of wisdom and kindness. They took the time to respond to an aspiring stranger, and I cannot thank them enough.

To Winzell, Cyndi, Riv, Kristen, Schuster, Vicki, Hannah, and all the others who've supported my journey, you all have been my inspiration to keep going when things weren't happening the way I'd planned. Special thanks to all of those who let me speak at events when I was just a college kid with a dream: Camille, Marcell, and many, many others.

Special thanks to Emily Barksdale who volunteered to edit the book. Without you, these words may have never seen the light of day. I owe you tremendously.

Most of all, thank you to the love of my life, the lovely Ms. Jessica Lauren Moore. Properly thanking you would require a whole 'nother book!

That's all for now,

—KEVIN L. MATTHEWS II

Made in the USA
San Bernardino, CA
29 August 2016